StartUp

Ken Beatty, Series Consultant

1

Sharon Goldstein
Kimberly Russell
Daria Ruzicka
Jenni Currie Santamaria
Kathleen Thompson

StartUp 1

Copyright © 2019 by Pearson Education, Inc.

All rights reserved. No part of this publication may be reproduced, stored in a retrieval system, or transmitted in any form or by any means, electronic, mechanical, photocopying, recording, or otherwise, without the prior permission of the publisher.

Pearson, 221 River Street, Hoboken, NJ 07030

Staff credits: The people who made up the StartUp team representing editorial, production, and design are Pietro Alongi, Peter Benson, Gregory Bartz, Magdalena Berkowska, Stephanie Callahan, Jennifer Castro, Tracey Munz Cataldo, Dave Dickey, Gina DiLillo, Irene Frankel, Héctor González Álvarez, Christopher Leonowicz, Bridget McLaughlin, Kamila Michalak, Laurie Neaman, Alison Pei, Jennifer Raspiller, Jeremy Schaar, Katherine Sullivan, Stephanie Thornton, Paula Van Ells, and Joseph Vella.

Cover credit: Front cover: Klaus Vedfelt/Getty Images. Back cover: Klaus Vedfelt/Getty Images (Level 1); Alexandre Moreau/Getty Images (Level 2); Matteo Colombo/Getty Images (Level 3); Javier Osores/EyeEm/Getty Images (Level 4); Liyao Xie/Getty Images (Level 5); Ezra Bailey/Getty Images (Level 6); guvendemir/Getty Images (Level 7); Yusuke Shimazu/EyeEm/Getty Images (Level 8); tovovan/Shutterstock (icons)

Text composition: emc design ltd

Library of Congress cataloging-in-publication data on file.

Photo and illustration credits: see pages 134–135

Printed in the United States of America

ISBN-10: 0-13-468413-3
ISBN-13: 978-0-13-468413-0

ISBN-10: 0-13-517846-0 (with app and Online Practice)
ISBN-13: 978-0-13-517846-1 (with app and Online Practice)

5 2022

ACKNOWLEDGMENTS

We would like to thank the following people for their insightful and helpful comments and suggestions.

Maria Alam, Extension Program-Escuela Americana, San Salvador, El Salvador; **Milton Ascencio**, Universidad Don Bosco, Soyapango, El Salvador; **Raul Avalos**, CALUSAC, Guatemala City, Guatemala; **Adrian Barnes**, Instituto Chileno Norteericano, Santiago, Chile; **Laura Bello**, Centro de Idiomas Xalapa, Universidad Veracruzana, Xalapa, México; **Jeisson Alonso Rodriguez Bonces**, Fort Dorchester High School, Bogotá, Colombia; **Juan Pablo Calderón Bravo**, Manpower English, Santiago, Chile; **Ellen J. Campbell**, RMIT, Ho Chi Minh City, Vietnam; **Vinicio Cancinos**, CALUSAC, Guatemala City, Guatemala; **Viviana Castilla**, Centro de Enseñanza de Lenguas Extranjeras UN, México; **Bernal Cespedes**, ULACIT, Tournón, Costa Rica; **Carlos Celis**, Cel. Lep Idiomas S.A., São Paulo, Brazil; **Carlos Eduardo Aguilar Cortes**, Universidad de los Andes, Bogotá, Colombia; **Solange Lopes Vinagre Costa**, Senac-SP, São Paulo, Brazil; **Isabel Cubilla**, Panama Bilingüe, Panama City, Panama; **Victoria Dieste**, Alianza Cultural Uruguay-Estados Unidos, Montevideo, Uruguay; **Francisco Domerque**, Georgal Idiomas, México City, México; **Vern Eaton**, St. Giles International, Vancouver, Canada; **Maria Fajardo**, Extension Program-Escuela Americana, San Salvador, El Salvador; **Diana Elizabeth Leal Ffrench**, Let's Speak English, Cancún, México; **Rosario Giraldez**, Alianza Cultural Uruguay-Estados Unidos, Montevideo, Uruguay; **Lourdes Patricia Rodríguez Gómez**, Instituto Tecnológico de Chihuahua, Chihuahua, México; **Elva Elizabeth Martínez de González**, Extension Program-Escuela Americana, San Salvador, El Salvador; **Gabriela Guel**, Centro de Idiomas de la Normal Superior, Monterrey, México; **Ana Raquel Fiorani Horta**, SENAC, Ribeirão Preto, Brazil; **Carol Hutchinson**, Heartland International English School, Winnipeg, Canada; **Deyanira Solís Juárez**, Centro de Idiomas de la Normal Superior, Monterrey, México; **Miriam de Käppel**, Colegio Bilingüe El Prado, Guatemala City, Guatemala; **Ikuko Kashiwabara**, Osaka Electro-Communication University, Neyagawa, Japan; **Steve Kirk**, Nippon Medical School, Tokyo, Japan; **Jill Landry**, GEOS Languages Plus, Ottawa, Canada; **Tiffany MacDonald**, East Coast School of Languages, Halifax, Canada; **Angélica Chávez Escobar Martínez**, Universidad de León, León, Guanajuato, México; **Renata Martinez**, CALUSAC, Guatemala City, Guatemala; **Maria Alejandra Mora**, Keiser International Language Institute, San Marcos, Carazo, Nicaragua; **Alexander Chapetón Morales**, Abraham Lincoln School, Bogotá, Colombia; **José Luis Castro Moreno**, Universidad de León, León, Guanajuato, México; **Yukari Naganuma**, Eikyojuku for English Teachers, Tokyo, Japan; **Erina Ogawa**, Daito Bunka University, Tokyo, Japan; **Carolina Zepeda Ortega**, Lets Speak English, Cancún, México; **Lynn Passmore**, Vancouver International College, Vancouver, Canada; **Noelle Peach**, EC English, Vancouver, Canada; **Ana-Marija Petrunic,** George Brown College, Toronto, Canada; **Romina Planas**, Centro Cultural Paraguayo Americano, Asunción, Paraguay; **Sara Elizabeth Portela**, Centro Cultural Paraguayo Americano, Asunción, Paraguay; **Luz Rey**, Centro Colombo Americano, Bogotá, Colombia; **Ana Carolina González Ramírez**, Universidad de Costa Rica, San José, Costa Rica; **Octavio Garduno Ruiz**, AIPT Service S.C., Coyoacán, México; **Amado Sacalxot**, Colegio Lehnsen Americas, Guatemala City, Guatemala; **Deyvis Sanchez**, Instituto Cultural Dominico-Americano, Santo Domingo, Dominican Republic; **Lucy Slon**, JFK Adult Centre, Montreal, Canada; **Scott Stulberg**, University of Regina, Regina, Canada; **Maria Teresa Suarez**, Colegios APCE, San Salvador, El Salvador; **Daniel Valderrama**, Centro Colombo Americano, Bogotá, Colombia; **Kris Vicca**, Feng Chia University, Taichung, Taiwan; **Sairy Matos Villanueva**, Centro de Actualización del Magisterio, Chetumal, Q.R., México; **Edith Espino Villarreal**, Universidad Tecnológica de Panama, El Dorado, Panama; **Isabela Villas Boas**, Casa Thomas Jefferson, Brasília, Brazil

LEARNING OBJECTIVES

WELCOME UNIT
page 2   In the classroom | Learn about your book | Learn about your app

Unit	Vocabulary	Grammar	Conversation/ Speaking	Listening
1 How's it going? page 5	• Meet and greet • Say hello and goodbye • Occupations • Things in an office • Countries	• Statements with *be* • Articles *a/an* • Regular plural nouns • *Need* and *have*	• Introduce yourself • Introduce others • Talk about things in an office **Skill** Ask someone to repeat a name	• Listen to an ad about things in an office **Skill** Listen for main ideas
2 Who are they? page 15	• Family relationships • Relationships • More family relationships	• Possessive adjectives • Questions with *who* and *what* • Negative statements with *be* • *Yes/no* questions with *be* • *Live* and *work*	• Identify family members • Talk about friends and family • Talk about where people live and work **Skill** Show interest	
3 What a beautiful home! page 25	• Places in the home • Places in the neighborhood • Things in the kitchen • Things in the house	• Adjective + noun placement • Prepositions of location • *There is/There are* • Questions with *where + be* • Prepositions of placement	• Describe your home • Describe your neighborhood • Talk about things in the home **Skill** Change the topic	• Listen to phone messages about a house **Skill** Listen for key words
4 Where are you now? page 35	• The calendar • Ways to connect • Words for getting around town	• Questions with *when + be* • Prepositions of time • The imperative: Affirmative and negative	• Ask about an event • Make plans with someone • Ask for and give directions • Say and repeat the time	• Listen to directions to the restaurant **Skill** Listen to follow directions
5 Do I need an umbrella? page 45	• Weather items • Weather and temperature • Seasons • Things you wear or carry	• Regular and irregular plurals	• Ask about prices • Talk about the weather • Talks about what people wear and carry • Say and confirm prices **Skill** Get someone's attention	• Listen to weather reports **Skill** Listen for specific information

KD_11.28.2022_1156

Pronunciation	Reading	Writing	Media Project	Learning Strategy
• Stressed words • Stressed syllables	• Read contact information **Skill** Skim	• Write contact information **Skill** Capitalize proper nouns	• Make a video about where you work or where you do your homework	**Vocabulary** • Use sticky notes
• The voiced *th* sound /ð/ • Linking words together	• Read about someone's family **Skill** Reread	• Write about your family **Skill** Form the possessive	• Describe photos of family and friends	**Vocabulary** • Learn related words
• The vowel /ə/ in unstressed syllables • Stress in compound nouns	• Read an ad for an apartment for rent **Skill** Use background information	• Write an ad for an apartment for rent **Skill** Write complete sentences	• Make a video about a room in your home	**Pronunciation** • Clap your hands
• The sound /ɚ/ • Stress in numbers	• Read about a plan to meet **Skill** Ask and answer questions	• Write about a plan to meet **Skill** Use end of sentence punctuation	• Describe photos of places and how to get there	**Grammar** • Make translation flashcards
• The letter *o* • Plural nouns	• Read messages about weather **Skill** Scan for details	• Write a message about weather **Skill** Use capitalization	• Make a video of your favorite clothes	**Vocabulary** • Make picture flashcards

Pronunciation	Reading	Writing	Media Project	Learning Strategy
• Weak pronunciation of *do* • Unstressed words	• Read a member profile **Skill** Compare and contrast	• Write a member profile **Skill** Write dates	• Make a video of a friend or family member doing something interesting	Vocabulary • Use action
• The vowels /i/ and /ɪ/ • Dropped syllables	• Read a restaurant review **Skill** Use context clues	• Write a restaurant review **Skill** Write commas in a list	• Make a video of your favorite meal	Vocabulary • Make word webs
• The sound /ʃ/ • Main stress	• Read about a hotel **Skill** Take notes	• Write about a hotel **Skill** Use abbreviations	• Describe photos of your neighborhood	Pronunciation • Practice the pronunciation
• Moving the main stress • Intonation in questions	• Read about computer problem **Skill** Make inferences	• Write about computer problems **Skill** Write a list	• Describe photos of your friends or family using technology	Grammar • Write the rule
• The simple past *-ed* ending • Blending *did you*	• Read about a vacation **Skill** Find the main idea	• Write about a vacation **Skill** Use commas	• Describe photos of a past weekend or vacation	Grammar • Write sentences

Key

 00-00 audio

 flashcards

 video

COACH video/coach

ActiveTeach

web search

TO THE TEACHER

Welcome to StartUp

StartUp is an innovative eight-level, general American English course for adults and young adults who want to make their way in the world and need English to do it. The course takes students from CEFR A1 to C1 and enables teachers and students to track their progress in detail against the Global Scale of English (GSE) Learning Objectives.

StartUp Level	GSE Range	CEFR	Description	StartUp Level	GSE Range	CEFR	Description
1	22–33	A1	Beginner	5	49–58	B1+	High intermediate
2	30–37	A2	High beginner	6	56–66	B2	Upper intermediate
3	34–43	A2+	Low intermediate	7	64–75	B2+	Low advanced
4	41–51	B1	Intermediate	8	73–84	C1	Advanced

English for 21st century learners

StartUp helps your students develop the spoken and written language they need to communicate in their personal, academic, and work lives. In each lesson, you help students build the collaborative and critical thinking skills so essential for success in the 21st century. *StartUp* allows students to learn the language in ways that work for them: anytime anywhere. The Pearson Practice English App allows students to access their English practice on the on the go. Additionally, students have all the audio and video files at their fingertips in the app and on the Pearson English Portal.

Personalized, flexible teaching

The unit structure and the wealth of support materials give you options to personalize the class to best meet your students' needs. *StartUp* gives you the freedom to focus on different strands and skills; for example, you can spend more class time on listening and speaking. You can choose to teach traditionally or flip the learning. You can teach sections of the lesson in the order you prefer. And you can use the ideas in the Teacher's Edition to help you extend and differentiate instruction, particularly for mixed-ability and for large and small classes.

Motivating and relevant learning

StartUp creates an immersive learning experience with a rich blend of multimedia videos and interactive activities, including interactive flashcards for vocabulary practice; Grammar Coach and Pronunciation Coach videos; interactive grammar activities; podcasts, interviews, and other audio texts for listening practice; humorous, engaging videos with an international cast of characters for modeling conversations; high-interest video talks beginning at Level 5; media project videos in Levels 1-4 and presentation skills videos in Levels 5-8 for end-of-unit skills consolidation.

Access at your fingertips

StartUp provides students with everything they need to extend their learning to their mobile device. The app empowers students to take charge of their learning outside of class, allowing them to practice English whenever and wherever they want, online or offline. The app provides practice of vocabulary, grammar, listening, and conversation. Students can go to any lesson by scanning a QR code on their Student Book page or through the app menu. The app also provides students with access to all the audio and video files from the course.

Components

For the Teacher

StartUp provides everything you need to plan, teach, monitor progress, and assess learning.

The *StartUp* **ActiveTeach** front-of-class tool allows you to

- zoom in on the page to focus the class's attention
- launch the vocabulary flashcard decks from the page
- use tools, like a highlighter, to emphasize specific text
- play all the audio texts and videos from the page
- pop up interactive grammar activities
- move easily to and from any cross-referenced pages

The interleaved **Teacher's Edition** includes

- an access code to the Pearson Practice English App and all digital resources
- language and culture notes
- teaching tips to help you improve your teaching practice
- *look for* notes to help assess students' performance
- answer keys to all Student Book exercises on the facing page of the notes
- and more!

Teacher's Digital Resources, all available on the Pearson English Portal, include

- Teacher Methodology Handbook
- A unit walkthrough
- ActiveTeach front-of-class software
- ExamView assessment software
- Teacher's notes for every Student Book page
- Rubrics for speaking and writing
- Hundreds of reproducible worksheets
- Answer keys for all practice
- Audio and video scripts
- The GSE Teacher Mapping Booklet
- The GSE Toolkit

For the Student

StartUp provides students with everything they need to extend their learning.

The optional **MyEnglishLab for *StartUp*** gives students more formal online practice and provides immediate feedback, hints, and tips. It includes

- grammar practice with remedial activities and access to all the Grammar Coach videos
- vocabulary practice, including games and flashcards
- speaking and pronunciation activities, including access to all the conversation videos and Pronunciation Coach videos
- listen-and-record practice that lets students record themselves and compare their recordings to models
- auto-graded reading and writing practice that reinforces skills taught in the Student Book
- summative assessments that measure students' mastery of listening, vocabulary, grammar, pronunciation, and reading
- a gradebook, which records scores on practice and assessments, that both students and you can use to help monitor progress and plan further practice

The optional *StartUp* **Workbook** provides practice of vocabulary, grammar, reading, and writing and includes self-assessments of grammar and vocabulary.

1 IN THE CLASSROOM

A Get to know your classmates

Play the Name Game.

B Classroom language

▶ 00-01 **Listen.**

Open your book to page 5.

Look at the picture.

Listen and repeat.

Read the title of this page.

Write your name.

Work in pairs.

Work in groups.

C Ask for help

▶ 00-02 **Listen.**

How do you say that in English?

How do you say that in English?

Desk.

Can you repeat that, please?

Can you repeat that please?

Sure. Desk.

How do you spell that?

How do you spell that?

D-e-s-k.

2 LEARN ABOUT YOUR BOOK

1. Look at pages iv–vii. What information is on those pages?

   _____

2. How many units are in the book? _____

3. How many lessons are in each unit? _____

4. Where is the grammar practice? _____

5. Look at the QR code [QR]. Find the icon on page 7. What does it mean? _____

   _____

6. Look at the ☐ I CAN STATEMENT at the bottom of page 7. What does it tell you? _____

   _____

7. Look at this icon 🔍. Find it on page 12. What does it mean?

   _____

3 LEARN ABOUT YOUR APP

1. Look inside the front cover. Where can you go to download the Pearson Practice English app for StartUp? _____

2. Where are the instructions for registering for the app? _____

   _____

3. Look at the picture of the app. What do you see?

   _____

4. Look at the picture again. Fill in the blanks with the numbers 1–3.
   a. Number _____ shows the practice activities.
   b. Number _____ shows the video files.
   c. Number _____ shows the audio files.

5. Look at the picture again. What does this ☁ mean? _____

   _____

6. Look at the QR code on page 7 again. What happens when you scan the code? _____

   _____

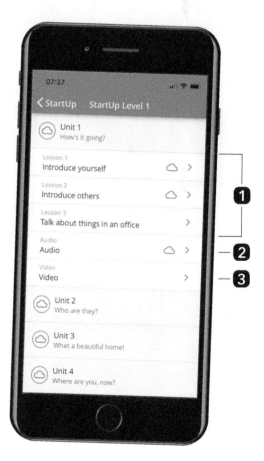

TSW MEDIA MEET THE PEOPLE OF TSW MEDIA

TSW Media is a big company with big ideas. It has offices all over the world. It works with international clients to help them market their products and services.

ESTER SILVA
Social media manager

▶ 00-03 Hey there. I'm Ester Silva. I work in the New York office. I'm the social media manager. I love to meet new people.

PEDRO CAMPOS
Photographer

▶ 00-06 Hey. I'm Pedro Campos. I am a photographer. I work in Mexico City. I always have my camera with me.

YUSEF SAYED
Lawyer

▶ 00-04 Hello. My name is Yusef Sayed. I'm married and I have two children. I'm from Dubai. I'm a lawyer and I travel a lot for work.

GABY RAMOS
Accounts manager

▶ 00-07 Hi! I'm Gaby Ramos. I live and work in Santa Cruz, Bolivia. I'm an accounts manager. I'm married and I love to hike in my free time.

TINA ADAMS
Illustrator

▶ 00-05 Hi there. I'm Tina Adams. I'm new! I just started my job. I work in the New York office. I'm an illustrator.

DAN LU
Graphic designer

▶ 00-08 Hello. My name is Dan Lu. I'm a graphic designer. I work in the Beijing office. I'm married and I have a new baby.

1 HOW'S IT GOING?

LEARNING GOALS

In this unit, you
- ⊘ introduce yourself
- ⊘ introduce others
- ⊘ talk about things in an office
- ⊘ read and write contact information

GET STARTED

A Read the unit title and learning goals.

B Look at the photo. What do you see?

C Now read Tina's message. Why is she happy?

TINA ADAMS
@TinaA

I'm so happy! I have a new job!

1 VOCABULARY Meet and greet

TINA ADAMS
@TinaA

There are so many new people here.

▶01-01 **Listen. Then listen and repeat.**

Hi. I'm Tom.

Hi. My name is Kate.

Nice to meet you.

Nice to meet you, too.

Handshaking
Shake hands with people when you first meet.

2 VOCABULARY Say hello and good-bye

▶01-02 **Listen. Then listen and repeat.**

Hi.

Hello.

Good morning.

How are you?

I'm fine. Thank you.

Fine, thanks. And you?

See you later.

Bye.

Good-bye.

Good night.

See you tomorrow.

3 LISTENING

A ▶01-03 **Listen. Circle a correct response.**

1. a. Nice to meet you.
   b. I'm fine, thank you.
2. a. Hi.
   b. Fine, thanks. And you?
3. a. Nice to meet you.
   b. See you later.
4. a. See you tomorrow.
   b. Nice to meet you, too.
5. a. Good-bye.
   b. Hello!
6. a. See you tomorrow!
   b. I'm fine. Thank you.

B ▶01-03 **Listen again and say a different response.**

4 PRONUNCIATION
COACH

A ▶01-04 Listen. Notice the stressed words. Then listen and repeat.
Good mórning.   Níce to méet you.   Whát's your náme?

Stressed words

We stress the important words in a sentence. Stressed words are strong and clear.

B ▶01-05 Listen. Circle the sentence with the correct stress. Then listen again and repeat.

1. a. Thánk you.
   b. Thank yóu.

2. a. Hów are you?
   b. How áre you?

3. a. Fine, thánks. And you?
   b. Fine, thanks. And yóu?

4. a. Góod night.
   b. Good níght.

5. a. Sée you later.
   b. See yóu later.

6. a. Whát's your náme again?
   b. What's yóur name agáin?

C PAIRS Check your answers.

5 CONVERSATION

A ▶01-06 Listen or watch. Number the sentences in the order you hear them.

___ How are you?
___ Nice to meet you.
_1_ Hello.
___ I'm sorry. What's your last name again?
___ Hi. I'm Tina Adams.
___ I'm fine.

B ▶01-07 Read the Conversation Skill. Listen or watch. Complete the conversation.

Ester: _____ . I'm Ester Silva.

Tina: _____ ! I'm Tina Adams. Nice to meet you.

Ester: I'm _____ . What's your last name again?

Tina: Adams.

Ester: Oh, OK. Adams. It's nice to meet you, too!

CONVERSATION SKILL
Ask someone to repeat a name

To ask someone to repeat a name, say, *I'm sorry. What's your name again?*
Listen or watch the conversation in 5A. Raise your hand when you hear someone ask to repeat a name.

I'm = I am

C ▶01-08 Listen and repeat. Then practice with a partner.

6 TRY IT YOURSELF

A MAKE IT PERSONAL Practice the conversation again. Use your own information.

B WALK AROUND Greet your classmates. Remember, you can ask your classmates to repeat their names.

☐ I CAN INTRODUCE MYSELF.

TINA ADAMS
@TinaA
I like my new neighbor.

 1 VOCABULARY Occupations

A ▶01-09 Listen. Then listen and repeat.

an architect

a manager

a chef

an engineer

a dentist

a flight attendant

a doctor

a programmer

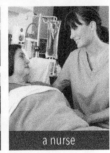
a nurse

a scientist

an accountant

an illustrator

B Label the pictures. Use words from 1A.

1.
2.
3.
4.
5.
6.
7.
8.

an architect _____ _____ _____ _____ _____ _____ _____

C TAKE A POLL Which occupation is the most interesting? The most difficult?
Which occupation pays the most?

2 GRAMMAR Statements with *be*; Articles *a / an*

COACH

Statements with *be*			Contractions	Articles	
Subject	***Be***			***A***	***An***
I	**am**		I**'m**	a student	an accountant
You	**are**	a doctor.	You**'re**	a teacher	an engineer
He	**is**		He**'s**	a programmer	an illustrator
She			She**'s**		
We			We**'re**	**Notes**	
You	**are**	doctors.	You**'re**	• Use *a* before nouns that start with a consonant sound.	
They			They**'re**	• Use *an* before nouns that start with a vowel sound.	
Note: Use contractions in speaking and informal writing.					

>> FOR PRACTICE, GO TO PAGE 105

3 PRONUNCIATION

A ▶01-11 Listen. Notice the stressed syllable in each word. Then listen and repeat.

stu·dent ar·chi·tect ac·coun·tant il·lus·tra·tor

B ▶01-12 Listen. Underline the stressed syllable. Then listen and repeat.

1. <u>doc</u>·tor
2. sci·en·tist
3. den·tist
4. man·a·ger
5. en·gi·neer
6. pro·gram·mer

C PAIRS Student A, say a word from 3B. Student B, point to the picture in 1A that matches the word.

> **Stressed syllables**
>
> Words are made up of syllables: tea·cher. One syllable in a word is stressed: tea·cher. The stressed syllable is strong and clear.

4 CONVERSATION

A ▶01-13 Listen or watch. Circle the correct answer.

1. Cole greets Tina with ___
   a. "Good morning."
   b. "Hi."
   c. "Hello."
2. Cole shows Tina ___
   a. the building.
   b. the kitchen.
   c. the office.
3. Ester says, ___
   a. "Thank you, Tina!"
   b. "Tina is a new illustrator."
   c. "Tina and I are old friends!"

B ▶01-14 Listen or watch. Complete the conversation.

> **Cole:** Tina, this is Ester. She's a social media _____ .
> And Ester, this is Tina. She's _____ .
>
> **Tina:** Hi, Ester. Nice to meet you.
>
> **Ester:** Hi, Tina. Nice to meet you, too.

C ▶01-15 Listen and repeat. Then practice with two partners.

5 TRY IT YOURSELF

A MAKE IT PERSONAL In groups of three, Student A, introduces Student B to Student C. Use your own names and occupations.

Lee, this is Carlos. He's an accountant. Carlos, this is Lee. He's a programmer.

B WALK AROUND Introduce your group to other classmates.

■ I CAN INTRODUCE OTHERS.

1 VOCABULARY Things in an office

TINA ADAMS
@TinaA

I need a lot of office supplies.

A ▶01-16 **Listen. Then listen and repeat.**

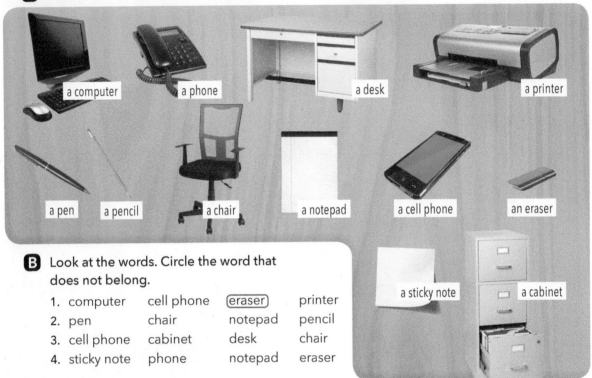

a computer   a phone   a desk   a printer

a pen   a pencil   a chair   a notepad   a cell phone   an eraser

a sticky note   a cabinet

B Look at the words. Circle the word that does not belong.

1. computer   cell phone   (eraser)   printer
2. pen   chair   notepad   pencil
3. cell phone   cabinet   desk   chair
4. sticky note   phone   notepad   eraser

C PAIRS Look around your classroom. Write a list of all the things in 1A that you see. Then compare your lists.

2 GRAMMAR Regular plural nouns; *Need* and *have*

COACH

Regular plural nouns

Singular	Plural	Notes
a phone an eraser	phone**s** eraser**s**	• Add **-s** to most regular nouns.
a box a class	box**es** class**es**	• Add **-es** to regular nouns that end in **s**, **x**, **z**, **ch**, or **sh**.
a dictionary a company	dictionar**ies** compan**ies**	• Change the **y** to **i** and add **-es** to nouns that end in a consonant + **-y**.
a shelf a life	shel**ves** li**ves**	• Change **f** and **fe** to **v** and add **-es** to nouns that end in **-fe** or **-f**.

Need, have

Subject	Need, have	Noun
I		
You	**need**	
We	**have**	a pen.
They		notepads.
He	**needs**	
She	**has**	

Notes
• Add **-s** to the base form of the verb for *he*, *she*, and *it*.
• *Have* is irregular. For *he*, *she*, and *it*, use *has*.

>> FOR PRACTICE, GO TO PAGE 106

3 LISTENING

A ▶01-18 Read the Listening Skill. Then listen. What is the main idea? _____

LISTENING SKILL Listen for main ideas

The first time you listen, don't try to understand every detail. Focus on the main idea.

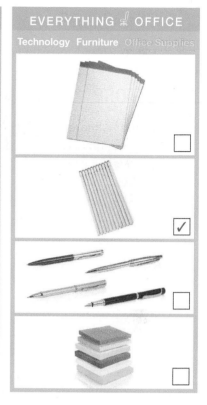

B ▶01-18 Listen again. Check (✓) the items you hear.

C GROUPS Close your books. What does Everything Office have? Make a list.

They have computers, printers ...

4 TRY IT YOURSELF

A TAKE A POLL Talk to three classmates. What do they have? What do they need?

	Need	Have
a pencil		✓ ✓ ✓
a cell phone		
a pen		
a notepad		
an eraser		
a computer		
a dictionary		

B CLASS Report to the class.

Three people have pencils ...

☐ I CAN TALK ABOUT THINGS IN AN OFFICE.

1 VOCABULARY Countries

▶01-19 Listen. Then listen and repeat.

TINA ADAMS
@TinaA
What is Ester's last name?

United States
France
China
Japan
Mexico
Brazil
Bolivia
United Arab Emirates
India

2 BEFORE YOU READ

Read the Reading Skill. Skim the information in the office directory. What is the purpose of the directory? It gives ___.

a. information about your family
b. information about yourself
c. technology information

3 READ

> **READING SKILL Skim**
>
> Skim means you read quickly to get the general or main idea. Don't read every word.

A ▶01-20 Listen. Read the contact information. What information do they have? Check (✓) all the correct answers.

☐ name ☐ email address ☐ job title ☐ office location
☐ age ☐ home address ☐ language ☐ phone number

ESTER SILVA
Social Media Manager

email
Ester.Silva@TSWmedia.com

office location
New York City, United States

phone
212 555-8575

TINA ADAMS
Illustrator

email
Tina.Adams@TSWmedia.com

office location
New York City, United States

phone
212 555-8205

PEDRO CAMPOS
Photographer

email
Pedro.Campos@TSWmedia.com

office location
Mexico City, Mexico

phone
011 52 555-4321

B ▶01-20 Listen again. How do we say "." and "@" in email addresses?

C Find Tina's, Ester's, and Pedro's offices on the map. Who works in the same office? _____

4 MAKE IT PERSONAL

> Find out about job titles. Research jobs and what they are called. 🔍

A Where do you keep your contact information? What information do you have for each contact?

B PAIRS Compare answers.

■ I CAN READ CONTACT INFORMATION.

1 FOCUS ON WRITING

A Read the Writing Skill.

B Read the directory on page 12 again.
1. Circle the capital letters at the beginnings of the proper nouns.
2. What are some kinds of proper nouns? Give examples.

WRITING SKILL Capitalize proper nouns

A proper noun is a specific person, place, or thing. Capitalize the first letter of a proper noun.

My friend Tina Adams works in New York at TSW Media.

2 PLAN YOUR WRITING

Imagine that you work for TSW Media. Think about a job you want to do. Then think about a city and country to live in.

3 WRITE

Write contact information for yourself. Include your name, job title, and the city and country where you work. Also include an email address, using this format "firstname.lastname@TSWmedia.com." Be sure to capitalize any proper nouns. Use the contact information on page 12 as models.

_____

_____

_____

email

_____

office location

_____

phone

_____

4 REVISE YOUR WRITING

A PAIRS Read your partner's contact information. Complete the chart.

Did your partner ...?	Yes	No
include name, job, city, country, and email address		
write the email address correctly		
capitalize proper nouns		

B PAIRS Can you improve your partner's contact information? Make suggestions. Then revise your writing.

5 PROOFREAD

Read your contact information again. Check your spelling, punctuation, and capitalization.

I CAN WRITE CONTACT INFORMATION.

PUT IT TOGETHER

1 MEDIA PROJECT

A ▶01-21 **Listen or watch. Answer the questions.**

1. What is Fumi's job?

   _____

2. Where is her office?

   _____

3. What is on her desk?

   _____

B **Make your own video.**

Step 1 Choose a place where you work or where you do your homework.

Step 2 Make a 30-second video. Introduce yourself. Talk about the place you work or study. Talk about the office items you have there.

Step 3 Share your video. Answer questions and get feedback.

2 LEARNING STRATEGY

> **USE STICKY NOTES**
>
> On sticky notes, write new vocabulary words. Put the notes on the items. Look at the notes and say the words.

Review the office vocabulary words in the unit. Make sticky notes for five things.

3 REFLECT AND PLAN

A Look back through the unit. Check the things you learned. Highlight the things you need to learn.

Speaking objectives
- [ ] Introduce myself
- [ ] Introduce others
- [ ] Talk about things in an office

Vocabulary
- [ ] Meet and greet
- [ ] Say hello and good-bye
- [ ] Occupations
- [ ] Things in an office
- [ ] Countries

Pronunciation
- [ ] Stressed words
- [ ] Stressed syllables

Grammar
- [ ] Statements with *be*
- [ ] Articles *a/an*
- [ ] Regular plural nouns
- [ ] *Need, have*

Reading
- [ ] Skim

Writing
- [ ] Capitalize proper nouns

B What will you do to learn the things you highlighted? For example, use your App, review your Student Book, or do other practice. Make a plan.

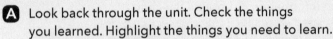

> ‹ Notes   Done
>
> In the app, watch the Grammar Coach video: Singular and plural nouns

2 WHO ARE THEY?

LEARNING GOALS

In this unit, you
⊘ identify family members
⊘ talk about friends and family
⊘ talk about where people live and work
⊘ read and write about families

GET STARTED

A Read the unit title and learning goals.

B Look at the photo of a family. What do you see?

C Now read Ester's message. What does she have on her phone?

ESTER SILVA
@EsterS

I have lots of family photos on my phone!

ESTER SILVA
@EsterS

My friend Pedro is here today.

1 VOCABULARY Family relationships

A ▶02-01 **Listen. Then listen and repeat.**

parents
mother   father
mom   dad

son

daughter

grandparents
grandfather   grandmother

grandson   granddaughter

sister   brother

B Look at the words in 1A. Complete the chart. Write family words in the correct column.

Male ♂	Female ♀	Male + Female ♂♀
father		

C PAIRS Show some family pictures. Say who they are.

2 GRAMMAR Possessive adjectives; Questions with *who* and *what*
COACH

Possessive adjective	Noun		Questions with *who* and *what*
My			*Who is = Who's*
Your			*What is = What's*
His	family	is happy.	**A:** ***Who's*** *that?*
Her			**B:** *That's my brother.*
Our	friends	are nice.	**A:** ***What's*** *his name?*
Your			**B:** *His name is Cole.*
Their			

Notes
- Use *its* for one thing.
  <u>TSW Media</u> is a big company. **Its** offices are in New York.
- Use *their* for more than one thing. <u>Those companies</u> are great. **Their** workers are nice.

>> FOR PRACTICE, GO TO PAGE 107

3 PRONUNCIATION

A ▶02-03 Listen. Notice the pronunciation of *th* in these words. Then listen and repeat.

The voiced *th* sound /ð/

To say the *th* sound in *that* and *they*, put your tongue between your teeth. Use your voice to make the *th* sound.

<u>th</u>at   <u>th</u>ey   mo<u>th</u>er   fa<u>th</u>er
Who's <u>th</u>at?   <u>Th</u>is is my bro<u>th</u>er.   <u>Th</u>at's her grandmo<u>th</u>er.

B ▶02-04 Look at each pair of words. Listen and circle the word you hear.

1. they / day   2. these / D's   3. these / Z's   4. they / day

C PAIRS Point to a photo in 1A. Explain who the people are.

In this photo there is a mother and father.

4 CONVERSATION

A ▶02-05 Listen or watch. Check (✓) all correct answers.

1. Who are Ester and Pedro talking about?
   ☐ Pedro's family   ☐ Ester's family   ☐ Pedro's mother

2. What family members do they talk about?
   ☐ father   ☐ sister   ☐ mother
   ☐ grandfather   ☐ brother   ☐ daughter

B ▶02-06 Listen or watch. Complete the conversation.

Ester: _____ that?

Pedro: That's my father.

Ester: Oh! _____ his name?

Pedro: His name is Eddy.

Ester: And who's that?

Pedro: That's _____ sister. Her name is Amelia.

C ▶02-07 Listen and repeat. Then practice with a partner.

5 TRY IT YOURSELF

A MAKE IT PERSONAL Ask and answer questions about your families. Use your photos.

A: Who's that?
B: That's my sister.
A: What's her name?
B: Her name is Mei.

B GROUPS Show your photos. Tell your group about your family.

This is my sister. Her name is Mei.
This is my son. His name is Bo.

☐ I CAN IDENTIFY FAMILY MEMBERS.

ESTER SILVA
@EsterS

Pedro takes great photos, and I do, too.

1 VOCABULARY Relationships

A ▶02-08 Listen. Then listen and repeat.

single | husband | married | wife | ex-husband | divorced | ex-wife

boyfriend | girlfriend | friends | co-workers

B ▶02-09 Listen. Then complete the sentences. Use words from 1A.

1. Tom is May's _boyfriend_ .
2. Lena and Luis are _____ .
3. Bill and Amy are _____ .
4. Ari is _____ .
5. Ken and Katy are _____ .
6. Pia is Ben's _____ .

C PAIRS Tell about five people you know or five famous people.

My sister is married. My friend David is single.

2 GRAMMAR Negative statements with *be*; Yes/no questions with *be*

COACH

Negative statements				Note: Use contractions in speaking and informal writing.
Subject	**Be**	**Not**		
I	am			I**'m not**
You	are			You**'re not** / You **aren't**
He She	is	not	Ester's friend(s).	He**'s not** / He **isn't** She**'s not** / She **isn't**
We You They	are			We**'re not** / We **aren't** You**'re not** / You **aren't** They**'re not** / They **aren't**

Yes/no questions			Short answers				
Be	**Subject**		**Affirmative**		**Negative**		
Are	you			I **am**.		I**'m not**.	
Is	he she	Ester's friend(s)?	Yes,	he **is**. she **is**.	No,	he**'s not**. / he **isn't**. she**'s not** / she **isn't**.	
Are	we they			we **are**. they **are**.		we**'re not** / we **aren't**. they**'re not** / they **aren't**.	

Note: Don't use contractions in affirmative short answers: *Yes, he is.* NOT ~~*Yes, he's.*~~

>> FOR PRACTICE, GO TO PAGE 108

3 CONVERSATION

 A ▶02-11 **Listen or watch. Circle the correct answer.**

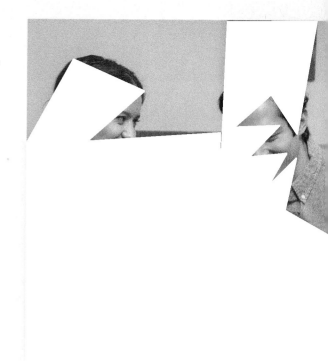

1. Ester's sisters are ___ .
   a. single
   b. married
   c. divorced
2. Ester's brother is ___ .
   a. single
   b. married
   c. divorced
3. Ester's brother is ___ .
   a. a doctor
   b. a programmer
   c. a student
4. Pedro is Ester's ___ .
   a. husband
   b. son
   c. boyfriend

 B ▶02-12 **Read the Conversation Skill. Listen or watch. Complete the conversation.**

Ester:	This is my family.
Pedro:	Really? _____ your sisters?
Ester:	Yes, _____ .
Pedro:	And _____ your brother?
Ester:	No, _____ . He's my boyfriend.

CONVERSATION SKILL
Show interest

To show interest, say:
- *Really?*
- *Is that right?*
- *Wow!*

Listen or watch the conversation in 3A. Raise your hand when you hear someone show interest.

C ▶02-13 **Listen and repeat. Then practice with a partner.**

4 TRY IT YOURSELF

 A MAKE IT PERSONAL Student A, show a photo of a person you know. Don't tell your partner who it is. Student B, ask 3-5 *yes/no* questions. Student A, answer your partner's questions with *yes* or *no*.

A: Is that your brother?
B: No. He's not my brother.
A: Is he a friend?
B: Yes, he is.

A: Is he married?
B: No, he isn't.
A: Is he a student?
B: Yes, he is.

B WALK AROUND Choose a different photo. Talk to five classmates. Ask and answer *yes/no* questions.

■ I CAN TALK ABOUT FRIENDS AND FAMILY.

ESTER SILVA

@EsterS

I miss my family. 😞 They live far away.

1 VOCABULARY More family relationships

A ▶02-14 **Listen. Then listen and repeat.**

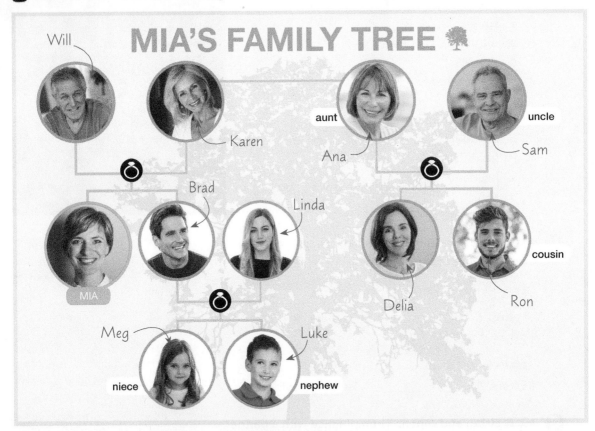

MIA'S FAMILY TREE 🌳

Will
Karen
aunt
Ana
uncle
Sam
Brad
Linda
MIA
Delia
cousin
Ron
Meg
Luke
niece
nephew

B Complete the sentences. Use words from 1A.

1. Luke is Mia's _nephew_ .
2. Sam is Mia's _____ .
3. Meg is Mia's _____ .
4. Ana is Mia's _____ .
5. Ron and Delia are Mia's _____ .

C PAIRS Draw a family tree and describe it.

This is my mother. Her name is Eva.

2 GRAMMAR Live and work

Subject	Live, work	
I You We They	live work	in New York City.
He She	lives works	

We use **and** to connect verbs or verb phrases in a sentence:
She lives and works in New York City.

>> FOR PRACTICE, GO TO PAGE 109

3 PRONUNCIATION

COACH

A ▶02-16 Listen. Notice the way we link a consonant to a vowel sound. Then listen and repeat.

I have a big family. This is my sister.
She lives in Miami. She works in an office.

Linking words together

We link words together when we speak. We link a word that ends in a consonant sound to a word that begins with a vowel sound.

B ▶02-17 Listen. Mark the consonant-to-vowel links. Then listen and repeat.

1. These are my parents.
2. They live in New York.
3. My brother lives in Canada.
4. He works at a university.
5. My aunt has a good job.
6. She's an engineer.
7. My cousin is an architect.
8. He works in London.

C PAIRS Practice saying the sentences in 3B.

4 CONVERSATION

A ▶02-18 Listen or watch. Check (✓) all correct answers.

1. Who lives in Brazil?
   - [ ] Ester's uncle
   - [ ] her sisters
   - [ ] her mother
   - [ ] her brother
   - [ ] her father

2. Who works for Super Cola?
   - [ ] Ester's sister
   - [ ] her sister's husband
   - [ ] her uncle
   - [ ] her aunt
   - [ ] her cousins

B ▶02-19 Listen or watch. Complete the conversation.

Ester: This is my uncle. He _____ in Florida, and he_____ for Super Cola.

Pedro: Really? Super Cola is a good company.

Ester: Yes, it is. My uncle is a general manager. He has three kids, and they all _____ there, too.

C ▶02-20 Listen and repeat. Then practice with a partner.

5 TRY IT YOURSELF

A MAKE IT PERSONAL Tell a partner about your family and friends.

A: My cousin lives in San José. He has two kids. He works for ABC Company.
B: Really? My friend Tom lives in San José.

B WALK AROUND Talk to five classmates. Tell your classmates about a friend or family member who lives and works in a different city.

■ I CAN TALK ABOUT WHERE PEOPLE LIVE AND WORK.

ESTER SILVA

@EsterS

My family gets together every year for a photo.

1 BEFORE YOU READ

How many people are in your family?
How would you describe them?

There are five people in my family—my parents, brother, and sister. My ...

2 READ

A ▶02-21 Listen. Read the email. What is it about? _____

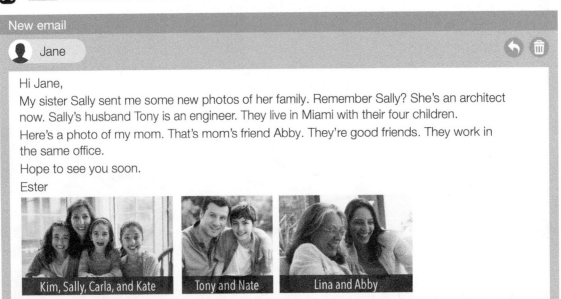

> **New email**
>
> 👤 Jane
>
> Hi Jane,
>
> My sister Sally sent me some new photos of her family. Remember Sally? She's an architect now. Sally's husband Tony is an engineer. They live in Miami with their four children.
>
> Here's a photo of my mom. That's mom's friend Abby. They're good friends. They work in the same office.
>
> Hope to see you soon.
>
> Ester
>
> Kim, Sally, Carla, and Kate | Tony and Nate | Lina and Abby

B Read the email again. Complete the sentences.

1. Sally is Tony's ____wife____ .
2. Lina is Sally's _____ .
3. Kim is Lina's _____ .
4. Lina is Nate's _____ .
5. Abby and Lina are _____ and _____ .

C Read the Reading Skill. Then read the email again. Answer the questions.

1. What does Sally do? _____
2. What does Tony do? _____
3. Where does the family live? _____
4. How many children do Tony and Sally have? _____
5. Where does Lina work? _____

> **READING SKILL Reread**
>
> Rereading a text can help you understand it better. Read the email once to learn what it is about in general. Then read it again to get more information.

3 MAKE IT PERSONAL

Find out about the family of a celebrity. 🔍

A Look at your family photos. Choose one and describe it.
Who are the people in the photo? What do they do? Where do they work?

B PAIRS Talk about the photo.

Taka is my brother. He's a lawyer.
He works in Osaka.

█ I CAN READ ABOUT SOMEONE'S FAMILY.

1 FOCUS ON WRITING

A Read the Writing Skill.

B Read the email on page 22 again. Circle the possessives.

WRITING SKILL Form the possessive

Add an apostrophe (') + s to a name or a noun to show possession.
Sally's family
My sister's husband

2 PLAN YOUR WRITING

A Choose three family members or friends. Complete the chart. Write information about each person.

Name: _____	Name: _____	Name: _____
Relationship: _____	Relationship: _____	Relationship: _____
Occupation: _____	Occupation: _____	Occupation: _____
Lives in: _____	Lives in: _____	Lives in: _____
Other: _____	Other: _____	Other: _____

B PAIRS Talk about each person. Use photos if possible.

That's my brother. His name is Tony. Tony's wife is a doctor.

3 WRITE

Write about your family. Include names, relationships, jobs, and where they live. Use the email on page 22 as a model.

4 REVISE YOUR WRITING

A PAIRS Read your partner's descriptions of his or her family. Complete the chart.

Did your partner ...?	Yes	No
describe his or her family		
use capitalization correctly		
form the possessive correctly		

B PAIRS Can you improve your partner's descriptions? Make suggestions. Then revise your writing.

5 PROOFREAD

Read your descriptions again. Check your spelling, punctuation, and capitalization.

■ I CAN WRITE ABOUT MY FAMILY.

PUT IT TOGETHER

1 MEDIA PROJECT

A ▶02-22 Listen or watch. Complete the chart about Rafael's friends.

	Location	Occupation	Single / Married
Leo			
Tom			
Lisa			
Frida			

B Show your own photos.

Step 1 Think about your family or friends. Choose or take photos of 4–6 people you know.

Step 2 Show the photos to the class. Talk about each person. Tell where they live, what they do, and if they are married.

Step 3 Answer questions from the class about your family or friends. Get feedback on your presentation.

2 LEARNING STRATEGY

LEARN RELATED WORDS

Some words are related. You can learn them in pairs. Write pairs of words that go together.

single / married
mother / father

Review the vocabulary words in the unit.
Write a list of words that are related.

3 REFLECT AND PLAN

A Look back through the unit. Check the things you learned. Highlight the things you need to learn.

Speaking objectives
- [ ] Identify family members
- [ ] Talk about friends and family
- [ ] Talk about where people live and work

Vocabulary
- [ ] Family relationships
- [ ] Relationships
- [ ] More family relationships

Pronunciation
- [ ] The voiced *th* sound /ð/
- [ ] Linking words together

Grammar
- [ ] Possessive adjectives
- [ ] Questions with *who* and *what*
- [ ] Negative statements with *be*
- [ ] *Yes/no* questions with *be*
- [ ] *Live, work*

Reading
- [ ] Reread

Writing
- [ ] Form the possessive

B What will you do to learn the things you highlighted? For example, use your App, review your Student Book, or do other practice. Make a plan.

> ‹ Notes   Done
>
> In the app, do the Lesson 2 vocabulary practice: Relationships

3 WHAT A BEAUTIFUL HOME!

LEARNING GOALS

In this unit, you
- ⊗ describe your home
- ⊗ describe your neighborhood
- ⊗ talk about things in the home
- ⊗ read and write an ad for an apartment for rent

GET STARTED

A Read the unit title and learning goals.

B Look at the photo of a home. What do you see?

C Now read Dan's message. Why is he in New York City?

DAN LU
@DanL

I'm working in New York City for three weeks and house-sitting for my friend Mike.

DAN LU
@DanL

The house is great. I start
working in New York City today.

1 VOCABULARY Places in the home

A ▶03-01 **Listen. Then listen and repeat.**

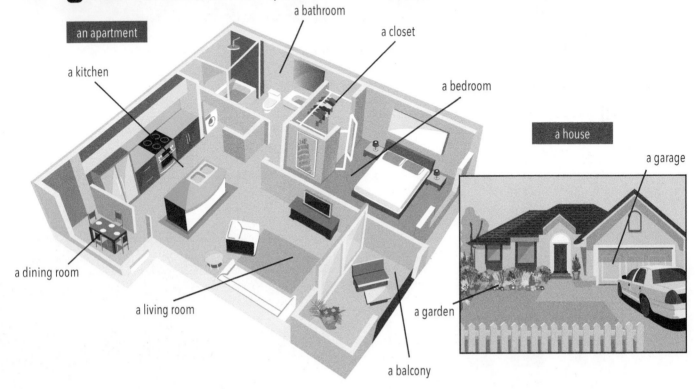

an apartment

a bathroom

a closet

a kitchen

a bedroom

a house

a garage

a dining room

a living room

a garden

a balcony

B ▶03-02 **Where are the people? Listen and circle the room.**

1. (a.) dining room   b. bathroom   4. a. bathroom   b. living room
2. a. bathroom   b. garage   5. a. kitchen   b. balcony
3. a. kitchen   b. bedroom   6. a. garden   b. closet

C PAIRS **Talk about your home.**

A: I live in an apartment. It has a kitchen, a living room, two bedrooms,
one bathroom, three closets, and a balcony.

B: I live in a house. It has a kitchen, a living room, three bedrooms,
two bathrooms, four closets, and a garage.

2 GRAMMAR Adjective + noun placement
COACH

Subject	Verb	Article	Adjective	Noun	Note: Adjectives do
It	is	a	small	apartment.	not change for plural nouns:
			nice	street.	*The house has big*
			pretty	garden.	*rooms.* NOT *The*
	has	a	new	kitchen.	*house has ~~bigs~~*
			large	living room.	*rooms.*

We use *but* to connect
ideas that show contrast:
*The house has a new
kitchen, but it has old
bathrooms.*

>> FOR PRACTICE, GO TO PAGE 110

COACH 3 PRONUNCIATION

A ▶03-04 Listen. Notice the short, quiet sound /ə/ in the unstressed syllables. Then listen and repeat.

kitchen   today   apartment   beautiful

> **The vowel /ə/ in unstressed syllables**
>
> The vowel in a stressed syllable is long and clear. Vowels in *un*stressed syllables often have the very short, quiet sound /ə/.

B ▶03-05 Listen. Underline the vowel that has the short, quiet sound /ə/. Then listen and repeat.

1. ga̱rage   2. closet   3. parent   4. office   5. balcony   6. tomorrow

C ▶03-06 PAIRS Listen. Complete the sentences. Then compare answers.

It's a beautiful _____ . It has a great kitchen, but no _____ .
It has a balcony, but no _____ .

D PAIRS Practice saying the sentences.

4 CONVERSATION

A ▶03-07 Listen or watch. Write the missing number.

1. Dan is in New York for _____ weeks.
2. The house has _____ bedrooms.
3. It has _____ bathrooms.

B ▶03-08 Listen or watch. Complete the conversation.

Cole:	Is the house nice?
Dan:	Yes, it is. It has a _____ living room.
Cole:	Oh yeah?
Dan:	Yeah, and a _____ dining room, _____ the bedroom is small.
Cole:	Oh, that's too bad.

C ▶03-09 Listen and repeat. Then practice with a partner.

D PAIRS Make new conversations. Use these words or your own ideas.

garden   garage
balcony   bathroom
kitchen   closet

5 TRY IT YOURSELF

A MAKE IT PERSONAL Talk more about your home.
Describe something you like and something you don't like.

A: I live in a house. It has a big living room, but it has a small kitchen.
B: My apartment has a nice balcony, but it only has one bathroom.

B WALK AROUND Tell three classmates about your home.

My house has two big bedrooms, but it has a small dining room.

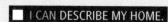 I CAN DESCRIBE MY HOME.

1 VOCABULARY Places in the neighborhood

DAN LU
@DanL

This is a beautiful neighborhood!

A ▶03-10 Listen. Then listen and repeat.

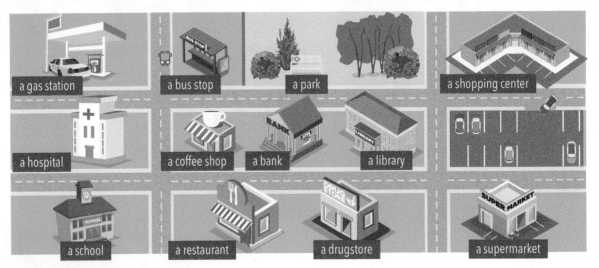

a gas station | a bus stop | a park | a shopping center
a hospital | a coffee shop | a bank | a library
a school | a restaurant | a drugstore | a supermarket

B Where do you find these things? Use words from 1A.

1. _a hospital_   2. _____   3. _____   4. _____   5. _____   6. _____

7. _____   8. _____   9. _____   10. _____   11. _____   12. _____

C PAIRS Which places from 1A are near your home? Make a list. Compare your lists.

2 GRAMMAR Prepositions of location; *There is / There are*

COACH

Look at the <u>bank</u> in the picture in 1A.

Prepositions of location		
	Preposition	**Noun**
It's	**across from**	the park.
	next to	the library.
	between	the library and the coffee shop.
	around the corner from	the supermarket.
	down the street from	the hospital.
	near	the bus stop.

There is / There are			
There	*Be*	**Noun**	
There	is	a park	near here.
	are	stores	

Notes
- *There is = There's*
- Don't contract *there are*.

>> FOR PRACTICE, GO TO PAGE 111

3 PRONUNCIATION

COACH

A ▶03-12 Listen. Notice the stress. Then listen and repeat.

bus stop   shopping center   drugstore   supermarket

> **Stress in compound nouns**
>
> A compound noun is a noun made up of two words, like *bus stop*. We usually stress the first word in a compound noun. We stress both words in an adjective + noun phrase, like *small house*.

B ▶03-13 Listen. Circle the compound nouns. Then listen and repeat the compound nouns.

1. a coffee shop
2. a great restaurant
3. a big room
4. a living room
5. a gas station
6. a new house

C PAIRS Check (✓) the places near your school. Then talk about them.

☐ coffee shop   ☐ bus stop   ☐ drugstore   ☐ gas station   ☐ supermarket

There's a bus stop and a gas station near my school.

4 CONVERSATION

A ▶03-14 Listen or watch. Circle the correct answer.

1. Tina is happy to be ___ .
   a. house-sitting   b. working   c. in the neighborhood
2. Tina likes ___ .
   a. libraries   b. big houses   c. parks
3. There are no ___ in the neighborhood.
   a. supermarkets   b. restaurants   c. parks
4. The bus stop is ___ the house.
   a. next to   b. across from   c. down the street from

B ▶03-15 Read the Conversation Skill. Listen or watch. Complete the conversation.

Tina:	So, I hear you're house-sitting in a big house?
Dan:	Yes, it's a great house and it's in a _____ neighborhood.
Tina:	Yeah? What's it like?
Dan:	There's a big park _____ the house.
Tina:	Sounds great.
Dan:	And there's a coffee shop _____ the park.

> **CONVERSATION SKILL**
> **Change the topic**
>
> Say *So* to change the way the conversation is going.
>
> Listen or watch the conversation in 4A. Raise your hand when you hear someone change the topic.

C ▶03-16 Listen and repeat. Then practice with a partner.

D PAIRS Make new conversations. Use these words or your own ideas.

shopping center
restaurant

5 TRY IT YOURSELF

A MAKE IT PERSONAL Talk about your neighborhood.

There's a restaurant near my apartment. There's a pharmacy down the street.

B WALK AROUND Talk to five classmates. Tell them about your neighborhood.

■ I CAN DESCRIBE MY NEIGHBORHOOD.

UNIT 3

1 VOCABULARY Things in the kitchen

DAN LU
@DanL

I can't find anything in this house!

A ▶03-17 **Listen. Then listen and repeat.**

a microwave

a cabinet

a pan

a pot

a cup

a glass

a fork   a knife   a bowl   a spoon

silverware   a plate

a stove / an oven

a sink

a refrigerator

a dishwasher

B Look at the words. Circle the word that does not belong.

1. stove   refrigerator   (cabinet)   microwave
2. microwave   fork   knife   spoon
3. cup   sink   bowl   glass
4. plate   pan   pot   dishwasher

C PAIRS Compare answers in 1B. Explain your choices.

2 GRAMMAR Questions with *where* + *be*; Prepositions of placement

COACH

Questions with *where* + *be*		Answers	Notes
Where	**is**	the cup?	**It's** in the sink.	• *Where is* = *Where's*
	are	the plates?	**They're** on the table.	• Don't contract *where are*.

Prepositions of placement		
The spoon is **in** the bowl. 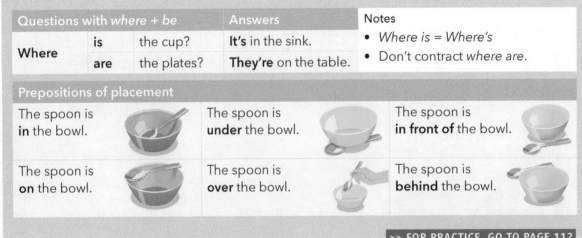	The spoon is **under** the bowl.	The spoon is **in front of** the bowl.
The spoon is **on** the bowl.	The spoon is **over** the bowl.	The spoon is **behind** the bowl.

>> FOR PRACTICE, GO TO PAGE 112

3 VOCABULARY Things in the house

A ▶03-19 Listen. Then listen and repeat.

a chair | a coffee table | a sofa

a dresser | a rug | a bed | a lamp

a bathtub | a shower | a toilet

B Write words that go in more than one room.

a chair – a dining room, a living room

C PAIRS Compare your answers in 3B.

4 LISTENING

A ▶03-20 Listen. Dan calls his friend Mike. Check (✓) all of the items Dan needs.

| _____ the kitchen table ☐ | over the ___sink___ ✓ | _____ the cabinet ☐ |
| next to the _____ ☐ | _____ the oven ☐ | under the _____ ☐ |

B ▶03-20 Read the Listening Skill. Listen again. Where are the items? Complete the locations in 4A.

C PAIRS Talk about the items in Mike's house.
A: Where are the pans? B: They're in the oven.

> **LISTENING SKILL Listen for key words**
>
> When you ask a question, focus on the key words in the answer. For example, if the question is *where*, listen for locations in the answer.

5 TRY IT YOURSELF

A MAKE IT PERSONAL Choose five items. Ask and answer questions about where you keep your kitchen items.
A: Where are your plates? B: My plates are in the cabinet.

B TAKE A POLL Choose one item. Ask five classmates: *Where is / are your ___?* Share the most common answer with the class.
Three people have a microwave over the stove.

■ I CAN TALK ABOUT THINGS IN THE HOME.

1 BEFORE YOU READ

Read the Reading Skill. Imagine you want to stay in an apartment. You look at ads online for vacation rentals. What questions do you want the ads to answer? Check the boxes.

- ☐ How many bedrooms does it have?
- ☐ What is the kitchen like?
- ☐ What is the neighborhood like?
- ☐ How much does it cost?
- ☐ Other? _____

DAN LU
@DanL

Visiting Chicago for a week.
Looking for a place to stay.

> **READING SKILL Use background information**
>
> Before reading a text, think about what you already know about the topic.

2 READ

A ▶03-21 Listen. Read the ad. Does it have the information you want? _____

Beautiful Downtown Apartment – Chicago, Illinois ★ ★ ★ ★ ★

Do you need a great place to stay in Chicago? It has one bedroom and one bathroom. The living room is large and sunny with a lot of windows and a balcony. You can see the whole city! It has a small kitchen, but the stove is new.

The apartment is close to stores and restaurants, and there's a bus stop across the street. There's a beautiful park around the corner. Stay here for a great time in Chicago!

No smoking   Check-in time: 3 p.m.
No pets   Check-out time: 11 a.m.

15 reviews

B Match the things on the left with their descriptions on the right.

1. kitchen
2. living room
3. stove
4. apartment
5. park

a. close to stores
b. around the corner
c. small
d. new
e. sunny

3 MAKE IT PERSONAL

Find a house-sharing website in the U.S. 🔍

A Would you like to stay in the apartment in the ad? Why or why not?

B PAIRS Compare your answers.

The apartment is small. I need two bedrooms.

☐ I CAN READ AN AD FOR AN APARTMENT FOR RENT.

1 FOCUS ON WRITING

WRITING SKILL Complete sentences

A sentence is a complete thought. It has a subject and a verb. Capitalize the first letter of the first word in a sentence.

A Read the Writing Skill.

B Read the ad on page 32 again. Circle the capital letters in the beginning of each sentence.

2 PLAN YOUR WRITING

A Label the pictures. Write details about the house and the rooms.

B PAIRS Talk about the home in the pictures.

The living room has big windows.   It has a nice kitchen.

3 WRITE

Write an ad for an apartment for rent, using the photos in 2A or your own home. Describe the rooms and tell what the home is like. Use the ad on page 32 as a model.

4 REVISE YOUR WRITING

A PAIRS Read your partner's ad. Complete the chart.

Did your partner ...?	Yes	No
describe the home		
capitalize the first word in a sentence		
capitalize proper nouns		

B PAIRS Can you improve your partner's ad? Make suggestions. Then revise your writing.

5 PROOFREAD

Read your ad again. Check your spelling, punctuation, and capitalization.

■ I CAN WRITE AN AD FOR AN APARTMENT FOR RENT.

PUT IT TOGETHER

1 MEDIA PROJECT

A ▶ 03-22 **Listen or watch. Answer the questions.**

1. What place does Pilar talk about? _____
2. Why does she like it? _____
3. What is in it? _____

B **Make your own video.**

Step 1 Choose a room in your home.

Step 2 Make a 30-second video. Talk about the room. Describe what is in it.

Step 3 Share your video. Answer questions and get feedback.

2 LEARNING STRATEGY

> **CLAP YOUR HANDS**
>
> To practice pronunciation, say a word and clap your hands on the stressed syllable.

Listen to the audio of compound nouns in the unit. When you hear the stressed syllable, clap your hands.

shopping center

3 REFLECT AND PLAN

A **Look back through the unit. Check the things you learned. Highlight the things you need to learn.**

Speaking objectives
- [ ] Describe my home
- [ ] Describe my neighborhood
- [ ] Talk about things in the home

Vocabulary
- [ ] Places in the home
- [ ] Places in the neighborhood
- [ ] Things in the kitchen
- [ ] Things in the house

Pronunciation
- [ ] The vowel /ə/ in unstressed syllables
- [ ] Stress in compound nouns

Grammar
- [ ] Adjective + noun placement
- [ ] Prepositions of location
- [ ] *There is / There are*
- [ ] Questions with *where + be*
- [ ] Prepositions of placement

Reading
- [ ] Use background information

Writing
- [ ] Complete sentences

B **What will you do to learn the things you highlighted? For example, use your App, review your Student Book, or do other practice. Make a plan.**

Notes   Done

In the app, watch the Lesson 1 conversation: Describe your home

_____
_____
_____
_____
_____

4 WHERE ARE YOU NOW?

LEARNING GOALS

In this unit, you
⊘ ask about an event
⊘ make plans with someone
⊘ ask for and give directions
⊘ read and write about a plan to meet

GET STARTED

A Read the unit title and learning goals.

B Look at the photo of a train station. What do you see?

C Now read Yusef's message. Why do you think he travels a lot?

YUSEF SAYED
@YusefS

I travel a lot for work. I'm always on a plane or a train!

YUSEF SAYED
@YusefS
I'm back in New York for work.

1 VOCABULARY The calendar

A Complete the words for the days of the week.

Sun_____   Mon_____   Tues_____   Wed_____   Th_____   Fri_____   Sat_____

B ▶04-01 Listen and check your answers. Then listen and repeat.

C ▶04-02 ▶04-03 Listen to the ordinal numbers and months on page 132.

D ▶04-04 Listen to the October dates. Then listen and repeat.

Write **October 17**.
Say *October seventeenth*

October

Sun	Mon	Tue	Wed	Thu	Fri	Sat
1	2	3	4	5	6	7
8	9	10	11	12	13	14
15	16	17	18	19	20	21
22	23	24	25	26	27	28
29	30	31				

E ▶04-05 Listen. Write the dates.

1. June 3_____
2. _____ 5
3. April _____

4. _____ 1
5. January _____
6. _____ 30

7. February _____
8. _____ 7
9. October _____

2 GRAMMAR Questions with *when + be*; Prepositions of time

Questions with *when + be*

When	**is**	the party?	**It's** at eight o'clock.
	are	the tests?	**They're** in the morning.

Note: In speaking and informal writing, use the contraction *When's*.

Prepositions of time

At	In	On	From ... to ...
at night	**in** 2019	**on** Sunday	**from** 8:00 **to** 9:00 P.M.
at noon	**in** May	**on** May 10	**from** March **to** April
at 9:30 P.M.	**in** the morning / afternoon / evening	**on** Tuesday, May 12	

>> FOR PRACTICE, GO TO PAGE 113

3 PRONUNCIATION

COACH

A ▶04-07 Listen. Notice that the underlined letters all have the same sound: /ɚ/. Then listen and repeat.

f<u>ir</u>st Th<u>ur</u>sday w<u>or</u>k thi<u>r</u>ty-f<u>ir</u>st

B ▶04-08 Listen. Circle the word that does *not* have the sound /ɚ/. Then listen and repeat the words with the sound /ɚ/.

1. thi<u>r</u>d   f<u>our</u>th   n<u>ur</u>se   thi<u>r</u>tieth
2. ci<u>r</u>cle   thi<u>r</u>teenth   m<u>or</u>ning   w<u>or</u>d
3. w<u>or</u>ld   b<u>ir</u>thday   t<u>ur</u>n   f<u>or</u>k
4. M<u>ar</u>ch   l<u>ear</u>n   h<u>er</u>   g<u>ir</u>l

> **The sound /ɚ/**
>
> We pronounce the sound /ɚ/ as one sound. This sound has several spellings. The most common spellings for /ɚ/ are *er* (h<u>er</u>), *ir* (f<u>ir</u>st), and *ur* (Th<u>ur</u>sday).

C ▶04-09 PAIRS Listen. Then practice saying these sentences.

His girlfriend works as a nurse.   Her birthday is March 31st.   She turns 30 on Thursday.

4 CONVERSATION

A ▶04-10 Listen or watch. Circle the correct answer.

1. Dan says to Yusef, ___ .
   a. "What's your name?"   b. "Great to see you!"   c. "How are you?"
2. Dan is in New York for ___ .
   a. a conference   b. a meeting   c. a new project
3. After New York, Yusef is going to ___ .
   a. London   b. San Francisco   c. Paris
4. Yusef is coming back to New York ___ .
   a. next week   b. in two weeks   c. in three weeks

B ▶04-11 Listen or watch. Complete the conversation.

Dan: _____ the conference?
Yusef: It's _____ October 15th to the 17th.
Dan: That's really soon.
Yusef: Yeah, it's from Tuesday to Thursday.
Dan: Oh, that's in two weeks.

C ▶04-12 Listen and repeat. Then practice with a partner.

D PAIRS Make new conversations. Use these words.

meeting   Wednesday to Friday   two days

5 TRY IT YOURSELF

A Imagine that there is a two-day meeting. Write notes.

Sept. 1–3,
Tues–Th

B ROLE PLAY Talk about the dates of the meeting.

A: When is the meeting?
B: It's from September 1st to 3rd, Tuesday to Thursday.

C WALK AROUND Continue the role play. Talk to five classmates. Use different events.

 I CAN ASK ABOUT AN EVENT.

YUSEF SAYED

@YusefS

It's 12 o'clock, is anyone free for lunch?

1 VOCABULARY Ways to connect

A ▶04-13 Listen. Then listen and repeat.

make a call

leave a voicemail message

send a text

send an email

have a video call

meet for lunch

talk on a break

have a meeting

B What's happening? Label the captions. Use words from 1A.

See you at the restaurant at 12:00.

Hi. This is Fumi. Can I speak to Taiki?

Everyone sit down please.

On my way home! ☎ ☺

Hi Dan. It's me Bob. Please call me back at 768-555-0987.

1. <u>meet for lunch</u> 2. _____ 3. _____ 4. _____ 5. _____

C PAIRS Talk about the ways to connect in 1A. Tell a partner which ones you do.

I text my friends everyday.

2 SPEAKING

A ▶04-14 Listen. Notice how we ask someone to repeat the time.
Then listen and repeat.

Let's meet at 4:00.

I'm sorry. What time?

4:00 o'clock.

Thanks.

12:00

twelve o'clock

12:30

twelve thirty

12:15

twelve fifteen

12:45

twelve forty-five

B ▶04-15 Listen to people making arrangements.
Write the number of the conversation in the correct column.

	Meeting	Lunch	Voicemail	Call	Video call	Break
conversation #					1	
time					4:15	

C ▶04-15 Listen again and write the time of each meeting in the correct column.

3 PRONUNCIATION

A ▶04-16 **Listen. Notice the different stress. Then listen and repeat.**

thirty   thirteen   forty   fourteen   sixtieth   sixteenth

B ▶04-17 **Listen. Circle the number you hear. Then listen and repeat.**

1. She's *80* / *⑱*.
2. He's *60* / *16* today.
3. It's in room *70* / *17*.
4. Is that on *40th* / *14th* Street?
5. It's at *2:50* / *2:15*.
6. It's on *June 30* / *June 13*.

C PAIRS Student A, say a number from 3A or 3B. Student B, write the number.

> **Stress in numbers**
>
> We stress the first syllable of numbers ending in *-ty* (or ordinal *-tieth*). We usually stress the last syllable of numbers ending in *-teen* (or *-teenth*).

4 CONVERSATION

A ▶04-18 **Listen or watch. Circle the correct answer.**

1. Yusef is leaving on ___ .
   a. Tuesday   b. Wednesday   c. Thursday
2. Yusef and Dan are going to ___ .
   a. an office   b. a restaurant   c. a park
3. Yusef leaves because he needs to ___ .
   a. go to a meeting   b. go to lunch   c. make a call
4. Dan doesn't know ___ .
   a. Yusef's phone number
   b. the name of the restaurant
   c. the time of the meeting

B ▶04-19 **Listen or watch. Complete the conversation.**

Dan: Are you free for _____ tomorrow?

Yusef: Sure! What time?

Dan: How about _____ ?

Yusef: Oh, I'm sorry. I have a meeting from _____ to _____ .

Dan: How about dinner?

Yusef: Perfect.

C ▶04-20 **Listen and repeat. Then practice with a partner.**

5 TRY IT YOURSELF

A MAKE IT PERSONAL **You want to arrange a meeting, lunch, or a video call with a co-worker. Take notes.**

What?	lunch
What day?	Wednesday
What time?	1:00

B ROLE PLAY **Imagine you and your partner are co-workers. Arrange a day and time to meet.**

A: Are you free for _____ on _____ ?
B: What time?
A: How about ... ?

■ I CAN MAKE PLANS WITH SOMEONE.

1 VOCABULARY Words for getting around town

YUSEF SAYED
@YusefS

How do I get to Putnam's?

A ▶04-21 Listen. Then listen and repeat.

avenue

street

a traffic light

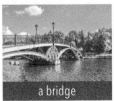
a bridge

a corner

a block

south

turn right

turn left

go straight

B ▶04-22 Listen to the conversations. Circle the correct answer.

1. (a.)   b.   4. a.   b.    7. a. Grant St.   b. Grant Ave.

2. a.   b.   5. a.   b.   8. a. 3rd St.   b. 3rd Ave.

3. a.   b.   6. a.   b.   9. a.   b.

C PAIRS Talk about places in your neighborhood.

A: There's a bridge on Third Street.
B: There's a bus stop on Oak Avenue. It's on the corner.

Places
shopping center
park
restaurant
drugstore
library
supermarket
coffee shop

2 GRAMMAR The imperative: Affirmative and negative

Affirmative	Negative	
Turn right.		**turn** left.
Walk.	Don't	**take** a cab.
Go north.		**go** south.
Cross the street.		**go** straight.

>> FOR PRACTICE, GO TO PAGE 114

3 LISTENING

A ▶04-24 Listen. Why is Dan calling Yusef? _____

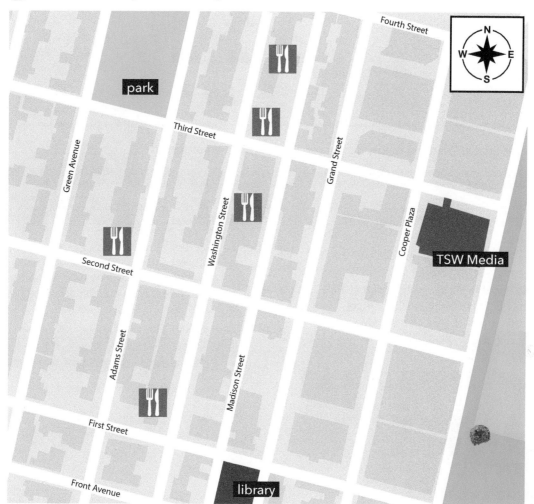

B ▶04-24 Read the Listening Skill. Listen again.
Start at TSW Media. Draw the route on the map.
Label Putnam's Grill.

C PAIRS Take turns asking for and giving directions
to Putnam's Grill. Student A starts at the park.
Student B starts at the library.

A: How do I get to Putnam's Grill? B: Walk ...

LISTENING SKILL
Listen to follow directions

When listening for directions,
focus on the direction words
and street names.

4 TRY IT YOURSELF

A MAKE IT PERSONAL Think of a place near your school. Draw or
find a map. Label your school, the streets, and show the direction
north. Write directions from your school to the place.

B PAIRS Student A, read the directions to the place. Student B,
follow the directions on your partner's map.
Point to the place. Guess where you are.

Turn left.
Walk three blocks south.
Cross the street.

☐ I CAN ASK FOR AND GIVE DIRECTIONS.

1 BEFORE YOU READ

YUSEF SAYED

@YusefS

I'm in New York this week. I can't wait to see my friend Nick.

Who do you make plans with? What do you do?

2 READ

A ▶04-25 Listen. Read the following emails. What is each email about? _____

New email		New email	
👤 Yusef Sayed	↩ 🗑	👤 Nick Johnson	↩ 🗑

Hi, Nick.
How are you and Sara? I'm in New York. Let's get together! Are you free for lunch on Saturday or Sunday? How about meeting at City Coffee at 1:30? It's on the corner of 8th Avenue and 13th Street. It's across from the supermarket. Just let me know.
I hope to see you!
Yusef

Hi, Yusef.
I'm free on Saturday. Sounds great! I know that place. The food is great, but the coffee is not so good. See you at 1:30.
All the best,
Nick

B Read the emails again. Write *T* for true and *F* for false.

____T____ 1. Yusef wants to meet for lunch.

_____ 2. Yusef and Nick are friends.

_____ 3. Nick can't meet on Saturday.

_____ 4. Nick needs directions to the coffee shop.

_____ 5. The coffee shop has great coffee.

C Read the Reading Skill. Write questions about the emails. Use *what, who, where, how,* and *when*. Then find the answers in the emails.

Who does Yusef want to meet?   Nick

_____   _____

_____   _____

_____   _____

_____   _____

> **READING SKILL**
>
> **Ask and answer questions**
>
> Ask yourself questions about the text. Then answer them to check your understanding.

🔍 Find out what year email started.

3 MAKE IT PERSONAL

A Do you use email to make plans with friends? with family? If not, how do you make plans?

B PAIRS Talk about how you make plans.

☐ I CAN READ ABOUT A PLAN TO MEET.

1 FOCUS ON WRITING

A Read the Writing Skill.

B Read the emails on page 42 again. Circle the question mark at the end of each question.

> **WRITING SKILL**
> **End of sentence punctuation**
>
> A sentence can be a statement or a question.
> End a statement with a period or an exclamation point.
>
> Use an exclamation point to express emotion.
> *It's great to see you again!*
>
> End a question with a question mark.
> *Are you free for lunch on Saturday?*

2 PLAN YOUR WRITING

A Choose a friend to make plans with. Imagine what you want to do. Decide where and when to do it. Complete the chart.

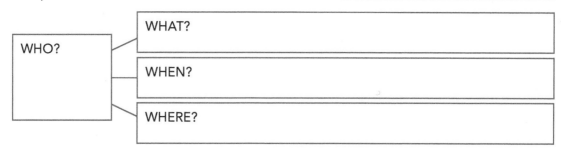

B PAIRS Talk about your plans.

I want to have lunch with ...   I want to go to ...

3 WRITE

Write to your friend. Invite your friend to meet you someplace. Suggest a day, a time, and a place. Use the email from Yusef on page 42 as a model.

4 REVISE YOUR WRITING

A PAIRS Read your partner's email. Complete the chart.

Did your partner ...?	Yes	No
invite a friend to meet		
suggest a day, time, and place		
use correct punctuation at the end of each sentence		

B PAIRS Can you improve your partner's email? Make suggestions. Then revise your writing.

5 PROOFREAD

Read your email again. Check your spelling, punctuation, and capitalization.

■ I CAN WRITE ABOUT A PLAN TO MEET.

PUT IT TOGETHER

1 MEDIA PROJECT

 A ▶04-26 **Listen or watch. Answer the questions.**

1. How does Lena go to school?

   _____

2. When does she have English classes?

   _____

3. Where does she go after school?

   _____

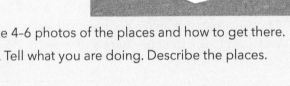

B Show your own photos.

Step 1 Think about what you do. Take 4-6 photos of the places and how to get there.

Step 2 Show the photos to the class. Tell what you are doing. Describe the places. Describe how to get there.

Step 3 Answer questions from the class about your daily activities. Get feedback on your presentation.

2 LEARNING STRATEGY

> **MAKE TRANSLATION FLASHCARDS**
> On a card, write a new word or phrase. On the back of the card, write a translation.

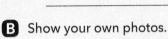

Review the grammar in Lesson 3. Make at least five translation flashcards for the imperative.

3 REFLECT AND PLAN

A Look back through the unit. Check the things you learned. Highlight the things you need to learn.

Speaking objectives
- ☐ Ask about an event
- ☐ Make plans with someone
- ☐ Ask for and give directions

Vocabulary
- ☐ The calendar
- ☐ Ways to connect
- ☐ Words for getting around town

Pronunciation
- ☐ The sound /ɚ/
- ☐ Stress in numbers

Grammar
- ☐ Questions with *when* + *be*
- ☐ Prepositions of time
- ☐ The imperative: Affirmative and negative

Reading
- ☐ Ask and answer questions

Writing
- ☐ End of sentence punctuation

B What will you do to learn the things you highlighted? For example, use your App, review your Student Book, or do other practice. Make a plan.

Notes · Done

In the app, listen to Listening 4A: Ask for and give directions.

5 DO I NEED AN UMBRELLA?

LEARNING GOALS

In this unit, you
- ⊘ ask about prices
- ⊘ talk about the weather
- ⊘ talk about what people wear and carry
- ⊘ read and write messages about weather

GET STARTED

A Read the unit title and learning goals.

B Look at the photo. What do you see?

C Now read Gaby's message. What are her plans?

GABY RAMOS
@GabyR

I'm in New York for two days for a meeting.

1 VOCABULARY Weather items

GABY RAMOS
@GabyR

Looks like rain. Where can I get an umbrella?

A ▶05-01 Listen. Then listen and repeat.

| an umbrella | a cap | gloves | a scarf | sunglasses |

| boots | a sweater | a coat | sandals | a raincoat |

B TAKE A POLL How many classmates have the items in 1A?

Four people have umbrellas. One person has a scarf. No one has sandals.

2 SPEAKING

A ▶05-02 Listen. Notice how you can ask someone to confirm or repeat information. Then listen and repeat.

How much is this, please?

It's 79 cents.

79 cents?

Yes. That's right.

Thanks.

	Under $1.00	$1.00–$1.99	Over $2.00
Write	6¢ or $.06	$1.06	$2.06
Say	six cents	a dollar six	two oh-six

B ▶05-03 Listen to people asking for prices. Write the number of the conversation in the correct box.

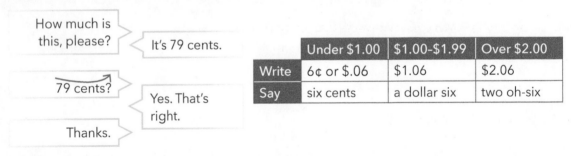

			1				
			$6.75				

C ▶05-03 Listen again. Write the prices.

3 CONVERSATION

A ▶05-04 **Listen or watch. Circle the correct answer.**

1. What does Gaby buy?
   a. water, gloves, and an umbrella
   b. water, a cap, and gloves
   c. gloves, an umbrella, and a scarf
2. What do Gaby and the clerk talk about?
   a. where things are
   b. the prices of things
   c. directions to a place
3. What's the total?
   a. $19.99
   b. $12.88
   c. $20.80
4. What do you think Gaby forgets?
   a. the bag
   b. the umbrella
   c. the water

B ▶05-05 **Read the Conversation Skill. Listen or watch. Complete the conversation.**

Gaby:	Excuse me.
Clerk:	Yes?
Gaby:	How much is this, please?
Clerk:	The water? It's _____ .
Gaby:	Oh! And how much are the gloves?
Clerk:	They're _____ .

CONVERSATION SKILL
Get someone's attention

Say *Excuse me* to get someone's attention in a store or restaurant.

Listen or watch the conversation in 3A. Raise your hand when you hear this expression.

C ▶05-06 **Listen and repeat. Then practice with a partner.**

D **PAIRS** **Make new conversations. Use these words or your own ideas.**

cap   boots

4 TRY IT YOURSELF

A ROLE PLAY **Imagine that you are in a store. Student A is a customer. Student B is a clerk. Student A, ask for prices. Use the things around you.**

A: Excuse me. How much is this pen?
B: It's ...

B WALK AROUND **Continue the role play. Talk to five classmates.**

1. Choose one thing around you.
2. Ask each classmate: How much is this?
3. Take notes.
4. Report back. $1.99 is the best price!

Pete — $1.99
Sue — $2.50

■ I CAN ASK ABOUT PRICES.

1 VOCABULARY Weather and temperature

GABY RAMOS
@GabyR

More traveling for work. I need to check the weather.

A ▶05-07 Listen. Then listen and repeat.

| sunny | partly cloudy | cloudy | windy | rainy | snowy |

B Look at the thermometer. Write *cold, cool, warm,* or *hot.*

1. It's 90° F or 32° C. It's _____hot_____ .
2. It's 30° F or 1° C. It's _____ .
3. It's 75° F or 24° C. It's _____ .
4. It's 60° F or 16° C. It's _____ .

C ▶05-08 Listen and check your answers. Then listen and repeat.

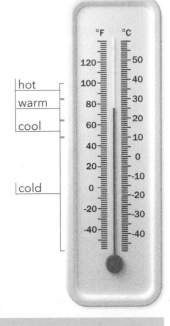

2 PRONUNCIATION

COACH

A ▶05-09 Listen. Notice the different vowel sounds.
Then listen and repeat.

/oʊ/	/ɑ/
c**o**ld	h**o**t
sn**o**wy	

/ʌ/	/aʊ/
c**o**me	cl**ou**dy

The letter o

The letter *o* usually has the sound /oʊ/ (n**o**) or /ɑ/ (n**o**t), but it can also have the sound /ʌ/ (c**o**me). The spellings *ow* and *ou* usually have the sound /aʊ/ (cl**ou**dy), but *ow* can also have the sound /oʊ/ (kn**ow**).

B ▶05-10 Listen. Notice the vowel sound. Complete the chart in 2A.
Write the words in the correct column. Then listen and check your answers.

sn**ow**y   br**ow**n   gl**o**ves   c**oa**t   d**o**llar   **o**ne   d**o**n't   n**o**t   h**ow**   h**o**me

C PAIRS Practice the conversation. Then make a new conversation.
Use words from 2A and 2B or your own ideas.

A: How's the weather at home?
B: It's cold and snowy. You need a coat and gloves.
A: Oh. It's hot and cloudy here. You don't need a coat.

3 LISTENING

A ▶05-11 Notice how we use *It's* to talk about the weather. Listen and repeat.

It's	sunny and nice.
	partly cloudy and 85°.
	cold and rainy and 45°.

Note: We also say *It's raining* and *It's snowing*.

LISTENING SKILL
Listen for specific information

You don't need to understand every word. Focus on the information you need. For example, for weather reports, listen for the weather words and temperatures.

B ▶05-12 Read the Listening Skill. Then listen to weather reports in six cities. For each city, write the weather words.

Denver _____

San Francisco _53°_ _cloudy, cool_ _____

Boston _____

Chicago _____

Houston _____

Miami _____

C ▶05-12 Listen again and write the temperatures.

D PAIRS Talk about the weather in each city.

4 VOCABULARY Seasons

A ▶05-13 Listen. Then listen and repeat.

FOUR SEASONS IN SEOUL

winter spring

summer fall

TWO SEASONS IN LIMA

the dry season

the wet season

B How many seasons does your city have? What are they? _____

C PAIRS When is the best time of year to visit your city? What is the weather like?
The best time to visit is in the …. It's ___ and ___ . It isn't ___ . It's about ___ degrees.

D WALK AROUND Tell three classmates your ideas.
Do you agree?

■ I CAN TALK ABOUT THE WEATHER.

GABY RAMOS
@GabyR

I'm meeting a new client for dinner. I think it stopped raining.

 1 VOCABULARY Things you wear or carry

A ▶05-14 Listen. Then listen and repeat.

Clothes   Shoes   Men   Women   Kids   Home   New

glasses
a top
a skirt

a backpack
shorts
a watch

a dress
a purse
shoes

a shirt
a jacket
a tie
pants

a T-shirt
jeans
socks
sneakers

B Look at the words. Circle the word that does not belong.

1. socks   shoes   (glasses)   sneakers
2. skirt   pants   sweater   tie

3. shirt   watch   top   T-shirt
4. purse   dress   umbrella   backpack

C PAIRS Compare answers in 1B. Explain your choices.

D GROUPS Answer the questions. Then report to the class.

Who wears jeans? Who wears a watch? Who wears ties?

In our group, five people wear jeans … One person wears a watch … No one wears ties …

 2 GRAMMAR Regular and irregular plurals

COACH

Regular plurals: Add -s or -es		Irregular plurals	
Singular	**Plural**	**Singular**	**Plural**
a shirt	shirt**s**	a woman	wom**e**n
a dress	dress**es**	a man	m**e**n
a lady	lad**ies**	a child	child**ren**
a scarf	scar**ves**	a person	**people**

Remember
- To form the plural of nouns that end in a consonant + **-y**, change the **y** to **i** and add **-es**.
- To form the plural of nouns that end in **-fe** or **-f**, change **f** and **fe** to **v** and add **-es**.

Note: *Jeans, pants, shorts,* and *glasses* don't have a singular form: *I wear ~~a short~~ shorts in the summer.*

>> FOR PRACTICE, GO TO PAGE 115

COACH

3 PRONUNCIATION

A ▶05-16 Listen. Notice the pronunciation of the plural -s and -es. Then listen and repeat.

<table>
<tr><td>no extra syllable:</td><td>sock ➜ socks</td><td>shirt ➜ shirts</td></tr>
<tr><td></td><td>shoe ➜ shoes</td><td>glove ➜ gloves</td></tr>
<tr><td>extra syllable /ɪz/:</td><td>dress ➜ dresses</td><td>watch ➜ watches</td></tr>
</table>

> **Plural nouns**
>
> We add an extra syllable /ɪz/ for the plural -s or -es after the sounds /s/, /z/, /ʃ/, /ʒ/, /tʃ/, and /dʒ/ (after the letters -s, -ce, -x, -z, -sh, -ch, -ge).
>
> We do not add an extra syllable after other sounds.

B ▶05-17 Listen. Circle the plurals that have an extra syllable. Then listen and repeat.

1. purses 2. jackets 3. phones 4. prices 5. scarves 6. bridges

C PAIRS Student A, say the singular form of a noun in 3A or 3B. Student B, say the plural.

A: jacket   B: jackets

4 CONVERSATION

A ▶05-18 Listen or watch. Circle the correct answer.

1. Bill and Gaby are meeting at 7:00 at ___ .
   a. a hotel   b. an office   c. a restaurant
2. Bill and Gaby talk about ___ .
   a. work   b. clothes   c. jokes
3. What is Gaby's problem?
   a. It's hot.   b. It's raining.   c. It's cold.
4. What does Gaby buy?
   a. a skirt   b. glasses   c. pants
5. What else does Gaby buy?
   a. a purse   b. a jacket   c. a hat

B ▶05-19 Listen or watch. Complete the conversation.

Gaby: I'm wearing _____ pants, a _____ shirt, and a _____ jacket.

Bill: And I'm wearing _____ pants, a _____ shirt, and a _____ jacket.

C ▶05-20 Listen and repeat. Then practice with a partner.

D PAIRS Make new conversations. Use these words or your own ideas.

jeans	shorts
cap	T-shirt
sweater	coat

5 TRY IT YOURSELF!

A MAKE IT PERSONAL Practice the conversation in 4B. Talk about what you are wearing.

B PAIRS Student A, describe what someone in your class is wearing. Student B, guess who the person is.

A: This person is wearing jeans, a red sweater, and sneakers.
B: Is it Robert?

■ I CAN TALK ABOUT WHAT PEOPLE WEAR AND CARRY.

LESSON 4　　READ MESSAGES ABOUT WEATHER

GABY RAMOS
@GabyR

Traveling to Tokyo, São Paulo, and Lima in March. What clothes do I need?

1 BEFORE YOU READ

Do you travel to other cities?
How do you find out about the weather there?

2 READ

> **READING SKILL** Scan for details
>
> Sometimes you need to find details or specific information. Read the text quickly. Don't read every word. Look for the details you need.

A Read the Reading Skill. Then read the questions. Scan the messages to answer the questions.

1. Which city is cool in March? _Lima_____
2. Which city is about 3°C in March? _____
3. Which city is rainy in March? _____
4. Which city is snowy in March? _____
5. Which city is not windy in March? _____

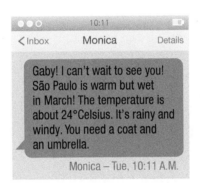

Kenji — Inbox — Details — 10:01

Hi, Gaby. I'm excited about your visit, too! Tokyo is cold in March! The temperature is about 3°Celsius. It's snowy and windy. You need a warm jacket, a hat, gloves, and boots.

Kenji – Tue, 10:01 A.M.

Monica — Inbox — Details — 10:11

Gaby! I can't wait to see you! São Paulo is warm but wet in March! The temperature is about 24°Celsius. It's rainy and windy. You need a coat and an umbrella.

Monica – Tue, 10:11 A.M.

Elias — Inbox — Details — 10:41

Gaby! I am so happy you are coming to Lima! In March, Lima is cool. The temperature is about 20°Celsius. It's cloudy. You need a sweater.

Elias – Tue, 10:41 A.M.

B ▶05-21 Listen. Read the messages. Write the city names next to what Gaby needs to take there.

Pack for _____
a sweater

Pack for _____
a jacket
a hat
gloves
boots

Pack for _____
a coat
an umbrella

> Find out about the weather in another city. 🔍

3 MAKE IT PERSONAL

A Choose a city you want to visit. Choose a month. List the things you need.

City: _____ Month: _____

Things I need:

_____ _____ _____

_____ _____ _____

B PAIRS Talk about your lists. Do you need the same things?

A: You need gloves in Toronto.
B: It's not cold in Mexico City. I don't need gloves …

■ I CAN READ MESSAGES ABOUT WEATHER.

1 FOCUS ON WRITING

A   Read the Writing Skill.

B   Read the messages on page 52 again.
Circle the months of the year.

> **WRITING SKILL Capitalization**
>
> Start months of the year with a capital letter. Don't capitalize the names of seasons. Look at these examples:
> *I like summer. July is my favorite month.*

2 PLAN YOUR WRITING

A   Complete the chart. Write a month and your city. Describe the weather and temperature. Suggest clothes to wear.

Month: _____

City: _____

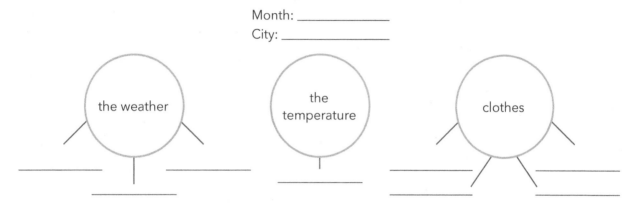

B   PAIRS Talk about the month you chose.   In June, the weather is ...

3 WRITE

Write a message to someone visiting your city. Describe the weather and temperature. Suggest clothes to match the weather. Use the messages on page 52 as models.

4 REVISE YOUR WRITING

A   PAIRS Read your partner's message. Complete the chart.

Did your partner ...?	Yes	No
describe the weather and temperature		
suggest clothes		
capitalize months of the year		

B   PAIRS Can you improve your partner's message? Make suggestions. Then revise your writing.

5 PROOFREAD

Read your message again. Check your spelling, punctuation, and capitalization.

■ I CAN WRITE A MESSAGE ABOUT WEATHER.

PUT IT TOGETHER

1 MEDIA PROJECT

 A  **05-22 Listen or watch. Answer the questions.**

1. What are Martin's favorite clothes?
   _____

2. What color is his jacket?
   _____

3. When does he wear his jacket?
   _____

B Make your own video.

Step 1 Choose some of your favorite clothes.

Step 2 Make a 30-second video. Describe the clothes.

Step 3 Share your video. Answer questions and get feedback.

2 LEARNING STRATEGY

> **MAKE PICTURE FLASHCARDS**
>
> On a card, draw a picture of a new word. On the back of the card, write a short sentence using the vocabulary word. Make 3-5 new cards every day. Review the cards twice a week.

It's a cloudy day.

Review the weather words in the unit. Make at least five picture flashcards.

3 REFLECT AND PLAN

A Look back through the unit. Check the things you learned. Highlight the things you need to learn.

Speaking objectives
- [ ] Ask about prices
- [ ] Talk about the weather
- [ ] Talk about what people wear and carry

Vocabulary
- [ ] Weather items
- [ ] Weather and temperature
- [ ] Seasons
- [ ] Things you wear or carry

Pronunciation
- [ ] The letter o
- [ ] Plural nouns

Grammar
- [ ] Regular and irregular plurals

Reading
- [ ] Scan for details

Writing
- [ ] Capitalization

B What will you do to learn the things you highlighted? For example, use your App, review your Student Book, or do other practice. Make a plan.

Notes   Done

Review the Writing Skill: Capitalization, page 53.

6 WHAT DO YOU LIKE TO DO?

LEARNING GOALS

In this unit, you
- ⊘ talk about music
- ⊘ talk about interests
- ⊘ talk about free-time activities
- ⊘ read and write a member profile

GET STARTED

A Read the unit title and learning goals.

B Look at the photo. What do you see?

C Now read Ester's message. What are her plans?

ESTER SILVA
@EsterS

Today we're having a party at work. Then I'm free for the weekend! 😊

ESTER SILVA
@EsterS

I hear music; time for the
birthday party. 🎈

 1 VOCABULARY Types of music

A ▶06-01 Listen. Then listen and repeat.

hip-hop

rock

pop

R&B (Rhythm and Blues)

dance music

classical music

jazz

country

B Think about artists and groups you know. Add more names to the chart.

Hip-hop	Rock	Pop	R&B
Eminem	U2	Jane Zhang	Beyoncé
Drake	Coldplay	Shakira	Bruno Mars

C PAIRS Compare your charts. Work together to add one more artist or group to each type of music. Name an artist for the other types of music in 1A.

A: I have Rihanna in R&B.   **B:** Really? I have her in pop.

 2 GRAMMAR Simple present: Affirmative and negative statements
COACH

Affirmative statements			Negative statements					Note: Use contractions in speaking and informal writing.
Subject	Verb		Subject	*Do / Does*	Not	Verb		
I You We They	like	jazz.	I You We They	do	not	like	rock.	*do not = don't* *does not = doesn't*
He She	likes		He She	does				

>> FOR PRACTICE, GO TO PAGE 116

3 CONVERSATION

 A ▶06-03 Listen or watch. Check (✓) the correct answers.

	Ester	Gaby	Ester and Gaby
1. Who likes cake?			
2. Who likes pop music?			
3. Who loves music?			
4. Who sings well?			

B ▶06-04 Read the Conversation Skill. Listen or watch. Complete the conversation.

Ester: What kind of music do you listen to?

Gaby: I _____ R&B.

Ester: Me, too. I _____ R&B!

Gaby: Who's your favorite artist?

Ester: I _____ Beyoncé! How about you?

Gaby: I don't know. There are so many.

> **CONVERSATION SKILL**
> **Ask someone the same question**
>
> Use *How about you?* to ask someone the same question the person asked you.
>
> Listen or watch the conversation in 3B. Raise your hand when the speaker asks the same question.

C ▶06-05 Listen and repeat. Then practice with a partner.

4 TRY IT YOURSELF

A MAKE IT PERSONAL Practice the conversation again. Talk about the music you like and don't like.

B WALK AROUND Ask four classmates about the music they like and don't like. Write their opinions in the chart.

Name	Likes (type of music + favorite artist or band)	Doesn't like (type of music)

C CLASS Report to the class.

Kara likes pop. Her favorite band is Exo. She doesn't like jazz.

■ I CAN TALK ABOUT MUSIC.

ESTER SILVA

@EsterS

Gaby, my co-worker, sings really well.

1 VOCABULARY Interests

A ▶06-06 Listen. Then listen and repeat.

play an instrument

play the guitar   play the piano

take pictures

write

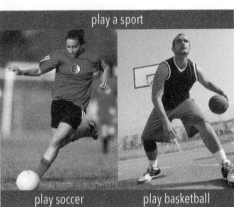

play a sport

play soccer   play basketball

cook

paint

dance

sing

swim

do martial arts

B Look at the words in 1A. Write the interests in the correct place.

play basketball _____   _____

(SPORTS)   (MUSIC)

_____   _____

_____

(ARTS)

_____

C GROUPS Student A, act out one of the interests from 1A. Others, guess the interest. Continue.

2 GRAMMAR Simple present: Yes/no questions and short answers

COACH

Yes/no questions			Short answers					
Do / Does	Subject	Verb	Affirmative			Negative		
Do	you they	cook?	Yes,	I they	do.	No,	I they	don't.
Does	he she			he she	does.		he she	doesn't.

>> FOR PRACTICE, GO TO PAGE 117

3 PRONUNCIATION

A ▶06-08 Listen. Notice the two pronunciations of *do*. Then listen and repeat.

/dəyə/   /dəyə/

Do you play a sport?   Yes, I do.   What do you play?

Weak pronunciation of *do*

In questions, *do* often has the short, weak pronunciation /də/. *Do you* often sounds like "d'ya" /dəyə/. *Do* does not have a weak pronunciation at the end of a sentence.

B ▶06-09 Listen. Circle the sentences where *do* has the weak pronunciation /də/. Then listen and repeat.

1. Do you like pop music?   3. Do you swim?   5. Do you?
2. Who do you like?   4. Yes, I do.   6. I do martial arts.

C PAIRS Ask and answer questions using *do* and the words in 1A.

4 CONVERSATION

A ▶06-10 Listen or watch. Circle the correct answer.
1. The *party / lunch / cake* is very good.
2. Gaby sings *in the kitchen / in the car / on the street*.
3. Ester loves to *dance / paint / sing*.
4. Gaby doesn't *dance / sing / cook* very well.

B ▶06-11 Listen or watch. Complete the conversation.

Ester: _____ an instrument?

Gaby: No, I don't. Do you?

Ester: I play the guitar a little. _____ though. Do you dance?

Gaby: No, _____ . But it's on my list.

Ester: Your list?

Gaby: You know, my list of all the things I want to learn!

C ▶06-12 Listen and repeat. Then practice with a partner.

D PAIRS Make a new conversation. Use these words or your own idea.   a sport   baseball   paint

5 TRY IT YOURSELF

A MAKE IT PERSONAL Practice the conversation again. Talk about your interests.

B WALK AROUND Find someone with each interest. Write the names in the chart.

cook	swim	do martial arts	play an instrument
play a sport	paint	dance	sing

C CLASS Report to the class.

 I CAN TALK ABOUT INTERESTS.

ESTER SILVA
@EsterS

Making new friends at the birthday party.

1 VOCABULARY Free-time activities

A ▶06-13 Listen. Then listen and repeat.

play board games

bike

hike

run

exercise

watch TV

read

go to the movies

listen to music

play video games

B Write words from 1A in the correct place.

Indoors	Both	Outdoors
play board games	run	hike

C PAIRS Imagine you are spending your free time together. Find two indoor activities and two outdoor activities that you both like. Underline the activities in 1B.

A: Do you play board games?
B: No, I don't. I play video games.
A: OK. Let's do that.

2 GRAMMAR Simple present: *Wh-* questions and answers

Questions				Answers
Wh- word	*Do / Does*	Subject		
What	do	you	**do** for fun?	I go to the movies.
Where	does	he	**swim**?	In the city pool.
When	do	they	**watch** TV?	In the evening.

>> FOR PRACTICE, GO TO PAGE 118

3 PRONUNCIATION
COACH

A ▶06-15 Listen. Notice the weak pronunciation of *to, for,* and *the.* Then listen and repeat.

I like to swim.   I read for fun.   I like to go to the movies.

> **Unstressed words**
>
> Important words in a sentence are stressed. Words like *to, for,* and *the* are usually *un*stressed and have a weak pronunciation. We say them quickly and quietly.

B ▶06-16 Listen. Complete the sentences. Use *to, for,* and *the.* Then listen and repeat.

1. I love _____ dance.
2. I like _____ listen _____ jazz.
3. I'm free _____ lunch.
4. I like _____ sing in _____ car.

C PAIRS Talk about what you do on the weekend.

A: *What do you do on the weekend?*   B: *I go to the gym. I like to exercise.*

4 CONVERSATION

A ▶06-17 Listen or watch. Circle the correct answer.

1. Ester goes dancing every ___.
   a. month   b. day   c. weekend
2. Gaby likes to ___ around the city.
   a. run   b. bike   c. hike
3. Ester swims on Tuesday and ___.
   a. Wednesday   b. Thursday   c. Friday
4. The swimming pool is ___.
   a. closed   b. new   c. open all night

B ▶06-18 Listen or watch. Complete the conversation.

Ester: _____ do you do for fun?

Gaby: I like to hike.

Ester: _____ do you go?

Gaby: The mountains. How about you? What do you like to do?

Ester: I like to swim.

C ▶06-19 Listen and repeat. Then practice with a partner.

D PAIRS Make new conversations. Use these words or your own ideas.   run   park   read

5 TRY IT YOURSELF

A MAKE IT PERSONAL What does your partner do for fun? Ask *what, where,* and *who* questions.

A: *What do you do for fun?*
B: *I like to run.*
A: *When do you run?*

B CLASS Report to the class.

■ I CAN TALK ABOUT FREE-TIME ACTIVITIES.

LESSON 4   READ A MEMBER PROFILE

ESTER SILVA
@EsterS
I found an online club.

1 BEFORE YOU READ

Imagine you want to join an online group.
What kind of information does a member profile have?

2 READ

A ▶06-20 Listen. Read the member profiles. What are they for? _____

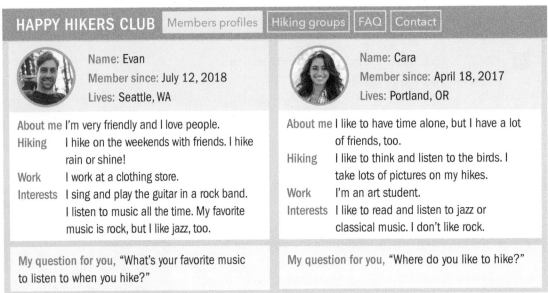

HAPPY HIKERS CLUB | Members profiles | Hiking groups | FAQ | Contact

Name: Evan
Member since: July 12, 2018
Lives: Seattle, WA

About me   I'm very friendly and I love people.
Hiking   I hike on the weekends with friends. I hike
            rain or shine!
Work   I work at a clothing store.
Interests   I sing and play the guitar in a rock band.
            I listen to music all the time. My favorite
            music is rock, but I like jazz, too.

My question for you, "What's your favorite music
to listen to when you hike?"

Name: Cara
Member since: April 18, 2017
Lives: Portland, OR

About me   I like to have time alone, but I have a lot
            of friends, too.
Hiking   I like to think and listen to the birds. I
            take lots of pictures on my hikes.
Work   I'm an art student.
Interests   I like to read and listen to jazz or
            classical music. I don't like rock.

My question for you, "Where do you like to hike?"

B Read the Reading Skill. How are Evan and Cara alike? Different?
Complete the chart with information from their profiles.

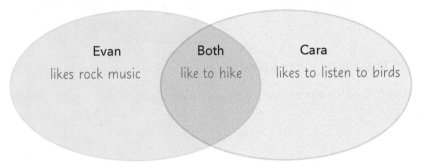

Evan
likes rock music

Both
like to hike

Cara
likes to listen to birds

READING SKILL
Compare and contrast

Read about two people
or things. How are
they alike? How are
they different? Use a
chart. This will help
you understand and
remember information.

C PAIRS Do you think Evan and Cara would like to hike together? Why or why not?

3 MAKE IT PERSONAL

Find a good place
near you to hike. 🔍

A Think about different kinds of groups. What kind of group do you want to join?

B PAIRS Discuss the groups you want to join. What do you want to see in a member's profile?
Talk about what you would like to know about the other members.

I want to join a cooking group …

☐ I CAN READ A MEMBER PROFILE.

LESSON 5   WRITE A MEMBER PROFILE

1 FOCUS ON WRITING

A Read the Writing Skill.

B Read the member profiles on page 62 again. Circle the dates.

WRITING SKILL Dates

For dates, we write the month first and then the day and year; for example:
January 5, 2018.

2 PLAN YOUR WRITING

A Imagine a kind of group to join. Create your member profile. Complete the chart with your ideas.

Kind of group: _____

Date you join: _____

What about you	Words that describe you	Interests
_____	_____	_____
_____	_____	_____

B PAIRS Talk about your profile.

I want to join a running club. I run ...

3 WRITE

Write your profile. Include the date you will join. Tell about yourself. Describe what you like and your interests. Use the profiles on page 62 as a model.

4 REVISE YOUR WRITING

A PAIRS Read your partner's profile. Complete the chart.

Did your partner ...?	Yes	No
write the date correctly		
describe what he or she is like		
include his or her interests		

B PAIRS Can you improve your partner's profile? Make suggestions. Then revise your writing.

5 PROOFREAD

Read your profile again. Check your spelling, punctuation, and capitalization.

☐ I CAN WRITE A MEMBER PROFILE.

PUT IT TOGETHER

1 MEDIA PROJECT

A ▶06-21 **Listen or watch. Answer the questions.**

1. When does Lucas take classes?

_____

2. What does Silvia do in her free time?

_____

3. When does she do it?

_____

B Make your own video.

Step 1 Think about the people you know. Who does something interesting in his or her free time?

Step 2 Make a 30-second video of the person doing that activity. Tell about it.

Step 3 Share your video. Answer questions and get feedback.

2 LEARNING STRATEGY

> **USE ACTION**
> Use actions to remember words. When you study, say the word and do an action. Review the words twice a week.

Review the activity words in the unit. Think of an action for each one. Say the word and do the action. Study three new words each day.

play the guitar

3 REFLECT AND PLAN

A Look back through the unit. Check the things you learned. Highlight the things you need to learn.

Speaking objectives
- ☐ Talk about music
- ☐ Talk about interests
- ☐ Talk about free-time activities

Vocabulary
- ☐ Types of music
- ☐ Interests
- ☐ Free-time activities

Pronunciation
- ☐ Weak pronunciation of *do*
- ☐ Unstressed words

Grammar
- ☐ Simple present: Affirmative and negative statements
- ☐ Simple present: *Yes/no* questions and short answers
- ☐ Simple present: *Wh-* questions and answers

Reading
- ☐ Compare and contrast

Writing
- ☐ Dates

B What will you do to learn the things you highlighted? For example, use your App, review your Student Book, or do other practice. Make a plan.

‹ Notes   Done

In the app, watch the Pronunciation Coach video: Unstressed words

_____
_____
_____
_____
_____

7 ARE YOU READY TO ORDER?

LEARNING GOALS

In this unit, you
- ⊘ talk about food
- ⊘ order in a restaurant
- ⊘ ask for restaurant items
- ⊘ read and write a restaurant review

GET STARTED

A Read the unit title and learning goals.

B Look at the photo of a restaurant. What do you see?

C Now read Pedro's message. What is he doing?

PEDRO CAMPOS
@PedroC

I'm meeting the New York photographer Lily for lunch today. She knows a great restaurant.

LESSON 1   TALK ABOUT FOOD

PEDRO CAMPOS
@PedroC

At Sam's Diner. I hope they have food I like!

1 VOCABULARY Food groups

A ▶07-01 Listen. Then listen and repeat.

FRUIT
- a banana
- an apple
- an orange

MEAT
- beef
- pork

VEGETABLES
- a potato
- an onion
- a carrot
- a tomato

POULTRY
- chicken
- turkey

DAIRY
- cheese
- milk
- butter

SEAFOOD
- fish
- shrimp

B What is your favorite:

vegetable? _____ fruit? _____ meat / poultry / seafood? _____

C PAIRS Compare answers.

A: Oranges are my favorite fruit, but I love apples and bananas, too.
B: I like oranges and apples, but I don't like bananas.

2 GRAMMAR Count / non-count nouns; *Some* and *any*

Count / non-count nouns		
Count nouns = things you can count	**Non-count nouns** = things you cannot count	**Note:** Non-count nouns take singular verbs.
one tomato	soup	*Cheese is my favorite food.*
two onions	butter	*The beef isn't good.*
five bananas	milk	

Some and *any*			Statements	
Yes/no questions			**Affirmative**	Yes, I have **some** milk.
Do you have	**any** **some**	milk? oranges?	**Negative**	No, I don't have **any** oranges.

Note: We usually use *any* in yes/no questions. We can also use *some* in yes/no questions when we offer or ask for something.

>> FOR PRACTICE, GO TO PAGE 119

3 PRONUNCIATION

COACH

A ▶07-03 Listen. Notice the different vowel sounds.
Then listen and repeat.

/i/ ch<u>ee</u>se m<u>ea</u>t b<u>ee</u>f turk<u>ey</u>
/ɪ/ ch<u>i</u>cken f<u>i</u>sh shr<u>i</u>mp a l<u>i</u>ttle b<u>i</u>t

B ▶07-04 Look at each pair of words. Listen and circle the word
you hear. Then listen and repeat.

1. eat / it   4. seat / sit
2. he's / his   5. these / this
3. leave / live

C PAIRS Practice the conversation. Use the foods in 3A.
A: Does the dish have ___ in it?   **B:** A little bit.   **A:** Oh. I don't eat ___ .

The vowels /i/ and /ɪ/

Notice the different vowel
sounds in m<u>ea</u>t /i/ and f<u>i</u>sh
/ɪ/. The sound /i/ (m<u>ea</u>t)
usually has a spelling
with e. The sound /ɪ/ (f<u>i</u>sh)
usually has a spelling
with i.

4 CONVERSATION

A ▶07-05 Listen or watch. Check (✓) all correct answers.

Pedro doesn't eat ___ .
☐ beef   ☐ carrots   ☐ pork   ☐ milk
☐ chicken   ☐ cheese   ☐ apples   ☐ onions

B ▶07-06 Listen or watch. Complete the conversation.

Pedro: Does the tomato soup have _____ in it?

Server: Yes, it does. There's milk in it. We have chicken soup.

Pedro: Oh … I don't eat meat.

Server: Oh. Well, how about _____ soup?

Pedro: Does it have any onions in it?

Server: Yes, it does.

C ▶07-07 Listen and repeat. Then practice with a partner.

D PAIRS Make new conversations. Use these words or your own ideas.
carrot   beef   tomatoes

5 TRY IT YOURSELF

A MAKE IT PERSONAL Plan an interesting dish. Use words in 1A.
Give it a name. What do you need to make the dish?
A: Let's make a chicken dish.
B: OK. We need chicken, an onion …

B CLASS Report to the class. Then vote on the most interesting dish.
Our dish is called "Grandma's Chicken." It has onions, a tomato, …

☐ I CAN TALK ABOUT FOOD.

LESSON 2   ORDER IN A RESTAURANT

PEDRO CAMPOS
@PedroC

Time to order. The servers here are very nice.

1 VOCABULARY Food and beverages

A ▶07-08 **Listen. Then listen and repeat.**

~ FOOD ~

a hamburger / a burger   a sandwich   pizza

salad   French fries   bread

pasta   rice

~ BEVERAGES ~

coffee   tea

soda   juice

B ▶07-09 **Listen to the descriptions. Write the food or beverage from 1A.**

1. ___pizza___   3. _____   5. _____   7. _____
2. _____   4. _____   6. _____   8. _____

C PAIRS **Find one food you both eat a lot of. Find one beverage you both drink a lot of.**

A: I drink a lot of coffee.
B: Me, too!

2 SPEAKING

A ▶07-10 **Notice how we order in a restaurant. Listen. Then listen and repeat.**

Can I take your order?

I'll have the chicken sandwich.

Anything to drink?

Yes, I'd like some coffee, please.

I'd like = I would like	I'll have = I will have
Use *the* to talk about items on the menu: I'll have *the* small salad.	

B ▶07-11 **Listen. Match the picture with the conversation. Write the number in the correct box.**

				1	
				I'll have	

C ▶07-11 **Listen again. Write *I'd like* or *I'll have* in the correct box in 2B.**

3 PRONUNCIATION

COACH

A ▶07-12 Listen. Notice the dropped syllable. Then listen and repeat.

favorite   vegetable   restaurant

Dropped syllables

Some words have a vowel that is not usually pronounced. When we don't pronounce the vowel, the word loses, or drops, a syllable.

B ▶07-13 Listen. Draw a line (/) through the vowel letter that is not pronounced. Then listen and repeat.

1. chocolate   2. every   3. different   4. family   5. business

C PAIRS Student A, say a word from 3A or 3B. Student B, say how many syllables you hear.

4 CONVERSATION

A ▶07-14 Listen or watch. Check (✓) all of the items that Lily orders.

Main dishes	Sides	Beverages
☐ hamburger	☐ French fries	☐ coffee
☐ chicken sandwich	☐ fruit salad	☐ hot tea
☐ fried fish	☐ tomato soup	☐ iced tea
☐ pizza	☐ baked potato	☐ soda
☐ garden salad	☐ cooked carrots	☐ juice

B ▶07-15 Listen or watch. Complete the conversation.

Server: Are you ready to order?

Pedro: Yes, I am. _____ the garden salad, please.

Server: And would you like something to drink?

Pedro: _____ some tea.

Server: Thank you. And for you?

Lily: _____ the hamburger.

C ▶07-16 Listen and repeat. Then practice with two partners.

D PAIRS Make new conversations. Use these words or your own ideas.

pizza   coffee   chicken sandwich

5 TRY IT YOURSELF

ROLE PLAY Imagine that you are in a restaurant. Student A, you are the server. Student B, you are the customer. Order food from 4A. Student A, write the order. Read it back to check that it is correct.

☐ I CAN ORDER IN A RESTAURANT.

PEDRO CAMPOS
@PedroC

Lily's right. The food here is good!

1 VOCABULARY Restaurant items

A ▶07-17 Listen. Then listen and repeat.

Menu

a napkin   a check   a tip

a menu   ice   sugar   salt   pepper   ketchup

B Write words that the sentences describe. Use words from 1A.

1. You put these on meat. _salt and pepper_
2. You put this in coffee. _____
3. You put this on French fries. _____
4. You put this in soda. _____
5. You use this to order food. _____
6. You get this at the end of a meal. _____
7. You leave this for the server. _____
8. You put this on your lap. _____

C GROUPS One person acts out using a word from 1A. The first person to guess correctly chooses a different word to act out.

2 GRAMMAR *Can* and *could* for requests; *Some* and *any* as indefinite pronouns

COACH

Can and could for requests				Answers
Can / Could	**Subject**	**Verb**		
Can **Could**	you	**bring**	some water, please?	Yes, of course.
	I	**see**	the menu?	Sure.
	we	**have**	the check?	No problem.
Note: *Could* is more polite than *can*.				

Some and any as indefinite pronouns
There's cake. Do you want **some**?
I'd like pasta, but they don't have **any**.
Note: Use *some* and *any* without a noun when it is clear what we are talking about.

>> FOR PRACTICE, GO TO PAGE 120

3 CONVERSATION

A ▶07-19 Listen or watch. Check (✓) all correct answers.

1. What does Pedro ask for?
   - [ ] water with no ice
   - [ ] a burger
   - [ ] a salad
   - [ ] some pepper
   - [ ] the check
2. What does Lily ask for?
   - [ ] water with ice
   - [ ] a napkin
   - [ ] ketchup
   - [ ] salt
   - [ ] a spoon

B ▶07-20 Read the Conversation Skill. Listen or watch. Complete the conversation.

Pedro: Excuse me. _____ some pepper, please?

Server: Yes, of course.

Pedro: Also, there's no ketchup. _____, too?

Server: Sure. Anything else?

Pedro: No, I think that's it. Thanks.

> **CONVERSATION SKILL**
> **Use polite expressions**
>
> When you ask for something, say *Please* and then *Thank you*.
>
> Listen or watch the conversation in 3A. Raise your hand when you hear someone use polite expressions.

C ▶07-21 Listen and repeat. Then practice with a partner.

D PAIRS Make new conversations. Use these words or your own ideas.

salt   sugar

4 TRY IT YOURSELF

A ROLE PLAY Prepare a funny skit. Student A, you are a new server. Students B and C, you are customers. There's nothing on the table. Customers, ask politely for the things you need.

B CLASS Present your skit to the class.

■ I CAN ASK FOR RESTAURANT ITEMS.

LESSON 4   READ A RESTAURANT REVIEW

PEDRO CAMPOS
@PedroC

Read my review of Sam's
Diner—great food and service.

1 BEFORE YOU READ

What kind of restaurant do you like?
What's your favorite lunch?

2 READ

A ▶07-22 Listen. Read the review. How does Pedro feel about Sam's Diner? _____

Sam's Diner

restaurant website

- map view
- nearby
- ★ save

Pedro Campos checks in to Sam's Diner 💬 ⚙

★★★★ May 12 at 12:30 P.M.

This is a great place to eat. It's in a convenient location
on a quiet street and close to the office.

They have a huge menu. There are many kinds of
sandwiches, soups, salads, and pastas. They also have
about twenty different kinds of pizza. The pizzas come
with lots of toppings like onions, chicken, and olives. My
favorite is pizza with salad on top! The service is excellent.
The servers are really friendly.

B Read the Reading Skill. Match the words with the meanings.

  _c_   1. convenient   a. a place
  ___   2. location   b. the help people give
  ___   3. huge   c. near or easy to get to
  ___   4. topping   d. very large
  ___   5. service   e. something you put on top of food

> **READING SKILL** Context clues
>
> To guess the meaning of an
> unfamiliar word, look at other
> words in the text around it.

C Read the review again. Choose the best answer.

1. Sam's Diner is ___ .
   a. far from the office   b. near the office   c. next to a park
2. Pedro likes a ___ place to eat.
   a. noisy   b. quiet   c. interesting
3. Pedro's favorite pizza has ___ on it.
   a. olives   b. onions   c. salad
4. The service at Sam's Diner is ___ .
   a. very good   b. very bad   c. just OK

3 MAKE IT PERSONAL

Find out about the
history of pizza. 🔍

A Describe a restaurant you really like.

B PAIRS Discuss what you like about your favorite restaurant.

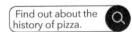
   ▉ I CAN READ A RESTAURANT REVIEW.

LESSON 5   WRITE A RESTAURANT REVIEW

1 FOCUS ON WRITING

A Read the Writing Skill.

B Read the review on page 72 again.
Circle the commas in the lists.

> **WRITING SKILL Commas in a list**
>
> A list contains three things
> (or more). We use commas to
> separate things in a list. Look at
> this example:
> *My favorite foods are pasta, pizza,
> and hamburgers.*

2 PLAN YOUR WRITING

A Think about a restaurant you like. Write the name. Then complete the chart.
Describe the location, food, and service. Complete the word webs.

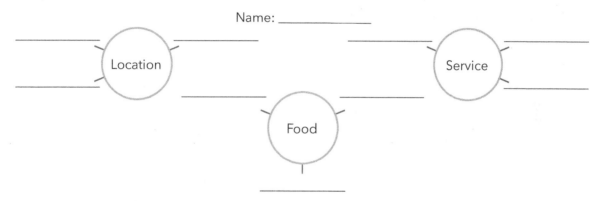

Name: _____

Location

Food

Service

B PAIRS Talk about the restaurant.
The restaurant is ...   They have ...

3 WRITE

Write a restaurant review. Talk about the location, food, and service.
Use the review on page 72 as a model.

4 REVISE YOUR WRITING

A PAIRS Read your partner's review. Complete the chart.

Did your partner ...?	Yes	No
describe the location		
describe the food and service		
use commas in a list		

B PAIRS Can you improve your partner's restaurant review? Make suggestions.
Then revise your writing.

5 PROOFREAD

Read your review again. Check your spelling,
punctuation, and capitalization.

■ ■ I CAN WRITE A RESTAURANT REVIEW.

PUT IT TOGETHER

1 MEDIA PROJECT

A 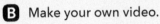 ▶07-23 **Listen or watch. Answer the questions.**

1. What is Ji-Ho's favorite food?

_____

2. Why does he like the restaurant?

_____

3. What is his favorite dish?

_____

B **Make your own video.**

Step 1 Choose a favorite restaurant or meal.

Step 2 Make a 30-second video. Talk about the meal. Describe what you eat and drink. Explain why you like it.

Step 3 Share your video. Answer questions and get feedback.

2 LEARNING STRATEGY

> **MAKE WORD WEBS**
> Word webs show how words are related. Put the main idea word in the center of a circle. Write related words around it.

butter _____

cheese _____   **DAIRY**   milk _____

Look at the food and restaurant vocabulary.
Make at least three word webs.

3 REFLECT AND PLAN

A Look back through the unit. Check the things you learned. Highlight the things you need to learn.

Speaking objectives
- ☐ Talk about food
- ☐ Order in a restaurant
- ☐ Ask for restaurant items

Vocabulary
- ☐ Food groups
- ☐ Food and beverages
- ☐ Restaurant items

Pronunciation
- ☐ The vowels /i/ and /ɪ/
- ☐ Dropped syllables

Grammar
- ☐ Count/non-count nouns
- ☐ *Some* and *any*
- ☐ *Can/could* for requests
- ☐ *Some* and *any* as indefinite pronouns

Reading
- ☐ Context clues

Writing
- ☐ Commas in a list

B What will you do to learn the things you highlighted? For example, use your App, review your Student Book, or do other practice. Make a plan.

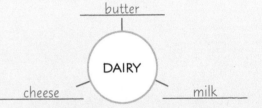

‹ Notes   Done

In the app, listen to Pronunciation 3A: Dropped syllables

_____

_____

_____

_____

_____

8 DO YOU HAVE A RESERVATION?

LEARNING GOALS

In this unit, you
- ⊘ ask for personal care items
- ⊘ give directions in a building
- ⊘ talk about where places are located
- ⊘ read and write about a hotel

GET STARTED

A Read the unit title and learning goals.

B Look at the photo of a hotel. What do you see?

C Now read Yusef's message. Where is he?

YUSEF SAYED
@YusefS

Finally at the hotel. I'm in San Francisco for a conference.

YUSEF SAYED

@YusefS

Bad luck—the airline lost my bag. ☹

 1 VOCABULARY Personal care items

 A ▶08-01 **Listen. Then listen and repeat.**

| body lotion | a toothbrush | shampoo | soap | conditioner | toothpaste |

| a comb | a brush | tissues | shaving cream | a razor | deodorant |

B Look at the words in 1A. Write the items in the chart.

Hair	Skin	Teeth	Shaving	Other
shampoo				

C PAIRS Compare answers.

 2 GRAMMAR *There is / There are*

COACH

Statements

Affirmative				Negative		
There	*Be*	**Subject**		*There*	*Be + not*	**Subject**
There	**'s**	some toothpaste	in the room.	**There**	**is not** / **isn't**	any toothpaste. / a toothbrush.
	is	a toothbrush				
	are	toothbrushes			**are not** / **aren't**	any toothbrushes.

Remember: Non-count nouns take singular verbs: *There is soap. There isn't any sunscreen.*

Yes/no questions			Short answers	
Be	*There*	**Subject**	**Affirmative**	**Negative**
Is	**there**	(any) toothpaste?	Yes, **there is.**	No, **there isn't.**
Are		(any) toothbrushes?	Yes, **there are.**	No, **there aren't.**

>> FOR PRACTICE, GO TO PAGE 121

3 PRONUNCIATION

A ▶08-03 Listen. Notice that the underlined letters have the sound /ʃ/. Then listen and repeat.

> **The sound /ʃ/**
>
> The sound /ʃ/ is usually spelled *sh*, but it has a few other common spellings (for example, *ti* and *ci*).

<u>sh</u>ampoo   <u>sh</u>aving cream   condi<u>ti</u>oner   lo<u>ti</u>on

B ▶08-04 Listen. Circle the word that does *not* have the sound /ʃ/. Then listen and repeat the words with the /ʃ/ sound.

1. toothbru<u>sh</u>   Engli<u>sh</u>   <u>ch</u>eck   <u>ch</u>ef
2. <u>s</u>ure   <u>sh</u>ower   <u>s</u>ugar   <u>s</u>unscreen
3. musi<u>ci</u>an   deli<u>ci</u>ous   <u>c</u>enter   so<u>ci</u>al
4. <u>sci</u>entist   direc<u>ti</u>ons   reserva<u>ti</u>on   pronuncia<u>ti</u>on

C PAIRS Say these sentences. Write one more sentence using words from 3A and 3B.

There's shampoo and conditioner in the shower.
I'm sure I have a toothbrush and shaving cream.

4 CONVERSATION

A ▶08-05 Listen or watch. Circle the correct answer.

1. Yusef is staying at the hotel for *two / three / four* nights.
2. He doesn't have *his room key / a reservation / his bag*.
3. He asks for *a razor / a brush / tissues*.
4. Yusef walks away because *he has everything / the clerk is busy / he is late*.

B ▶08-06 Listen or watch. Complete the conversation.

Yusef:	I don't have a toothbrush or toothpaste.
Clerk:	_____ toothpaste in the back.
Yusef:	_____ combs back there?
Clerk:	I'm sure there are. Let me check.
Yusef:	Thank you.
Clerk:	Here you go! I think we have everything you need. And of course _____ shampoo in the room.

C ▶08-07 Listen and repeat. Then practice with a partner.

D PAIRS Make a new conversation. Use these words or your own ideas.

shaving cream   razors   soap

5 TRY IT YOURSELF

A MAKE IT PERSONAL Look at the personal care items in 1A. Make one list of six items you need and one list of six items you don't need. Don't show your lists to your partner.

B ROLE PLAY Imagine you are in the same family. Student A, you are going to the drugstore. Ask Student B which items to buy.

A: Is there any shampoo?
B: No, there isn't. We need shampoo.

■ I CAN ASK FOR PERSONAL CARE ITEMS.

YUSEF SAYED

@YusefS

This hotel is so big! I can't find anything.

1 VOCABULARY Places in a hotel

A ▶08-08 **Listen. Then listen and repeat.**

a parking lot

a café

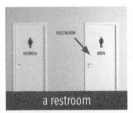
a restroom

a fitness center

a pool

a gift shop

a business center

a sauna

a lobby

an escalator

an elevator

B Write the place next to the activity. Use words from 1A.

1. eat lunch _a café_____
2. go swimming _____
3. buy a T-shirt _____
4. leave your car _____
5. use the internet _____
6. exercise _____
7. go up to your room _____ / _____

C PAIRS Compare your answers.

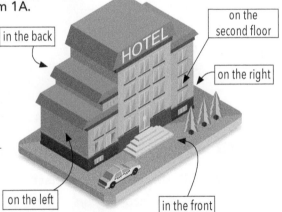

in the back

on the second floor

on the right

on the left

in the front

2 GRAMMAR Like, want, need + infinitives

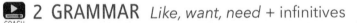

Affirmative statements			Negative statements				Notes
Subject	Verb	Infinitive	Subject	*Do not*	Verb	Infinitive	• Infinitive = *to* + base form of the verb.
I You We They	like want need	to travel.	I You We They	do not	like want need	to travel.	• Use contractions in speaking and informal writing.
He She	likes wants needs		He She	does not	like want need		

>> FOR PRACTICE, GO TO PAGE 122

3 PRONUNCIATION
COACH

A ▶08-10 Listen. Notice the main stress. Then listen and repeat.
Where's the fĭtness center?   Take the ĕlevator.   It's on the lĕft.

Main stress

We stress the important words in a sentence. One word has the main (strongest) stress. The main stress is often on the last important word.

B ▶08-11 Listen. Underline the word that has the main stress. Then listen and repeat.

1. A: How can I help you?
   B: Where's the sauna?
   A: It's next to the pool.

2. A: Where's the gift shop?
   B: It's right over there.
   A: Right, I see it.

C PAIRS Practice the conversations in 3B.

4 CONVERSATION

 A ▶08-12 Listen or watch. Circle the correct answer.

1. Yusef thanks the clerk for his *help / time / call*.
2. Yusef wants to *eat / sleep / watch TV*.
3. The business center is next to the *pool / café / gift shop*.
4. The elevators are *on the right / on the left / in front* of Yusef.

  B ▶08-13 Read the Conversation Skill. Listen or watch. Complete the conversation.

Yusef: Where is the café?

Clerk: It's _____ .

Yusef: I see. Do you have a fitness center?
        I _____ before dinner, tonight.

Clerk: Yes, we do. It's on the top floor.

Yusef: Thanks. And I _____ something.
        Where's the business center?

Clerk: It's over there, on the right.

CONVERSATION SKILL
Show understanding

To show that you understand what someone is saying, say:
- *I see.*
- *Uh-huh.*
- *Right.*

Listen or watch the conversation in 4A. Raise your hand when the speaker shows understanding.

C ▶08-14 Listen and repeat. Then practice with a partner.

D PAIRS Make a new conversation. Use these words or your own ideas.

gift shop
pool
on the left

5 TRY IT YOURSELF

ROLE PLAY **Look at the floor plans. Ask for and give directions.**

A: Excuse me. Is there a business center here? I want to use a computer.

B: Yes, there is. Take the elevator to the second floor. The business center is on the right.

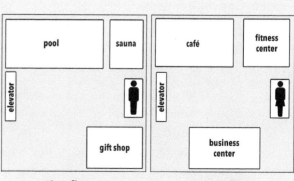

First floor   **Second floor**

■ I CAN GIVE DIRECTIONS IN A BUILDING.

YUSEF SAYED
@YusefS

I have the afternoon free.
Time to see San Francisco!

 1 VOCABULARY Places in a city

A ▶08-15 **Listen. Then listen and repeat.**

a stadium

an art gallery

a subway station

a museum

a theater

an ATM / a bank

a convenience store

a post office

a department store

an airport

a hair salon

a club

B Look at the words in 1A. Complete the chart.

Transportation	Shopping	Entertainment / Culture	Services
a subway station			

C PAIRS Compare answers.

2 GRAMMAR Prepositions of place: *At, on, in*

At	On	In
at work	**on** the street	**in** Japan
at home	**on** the corner	**in** New York
at school	**on** Main Street	**in** the park
at the library	**on** the left	**in** the neighborhood
at a bus stop	**on** the right	**in** the front
at 10 Main Street	**on** the second floor	**in** the back

>> FOR PRACTICE, GO TO PAGE 123

3 LISTENING

A ▶08-17 Listen. Yusef is using his phone to find locations. Check (✓) the places he wants to go.

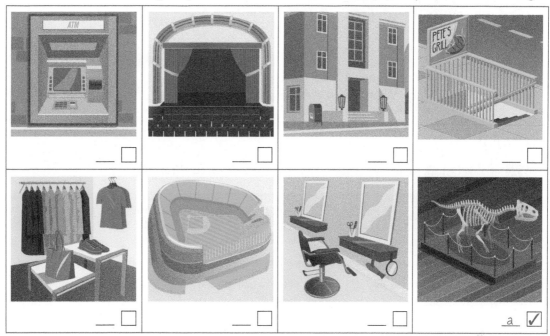

B ▶08-17 Read the Listening Skill. Read the locations.
Then listen again and write the letter under the place in 3A.

a. in Golden Gate Park
b. on Second Street
c. on Market Street
d. on the corner
e. at 6911 O'Farrell Street
f. at 6911 Fell Street

> **LISTENING SKILL** Listen for location words
>
> When you ask for a location, focus on the key words in the answer. For example, listen carefully for address numbers and street names.

C PAIRS Talk about the location of the places in 3A.
A: Where is the museum?
B: It's in Golden Gate Park.

4 TRY IT YOURSELF

A MAKE IT PERSONAL Make a list of 5–10 places that are nearby or famous in your city.

B ROLE PLAY Imagine that you are a visitor to your city. Take turns.
Ask where the places on your list are.
A: Where is the Modern Art Museum?
B: It's on Grant Street.

■ I CAN TALK ABOUT WHERE PLACES ARE LOCATED.

YUSEF SAYED

@YusefS

Anyone need a great hotel in San Francisco? Try the Grand.

1 BEFORE YOU READ

Imagine you need to choose a hotel for a business conference. What things are important to you?

2 READ

A ▶08-18 Listen. Read the email. Why is Yusef writing to Gina? _____

> **Yusef Sayed**
>
> Hi, Gina,
>
> I have an idea for our conference in September in San Francisco. I think the Grand Hotel is perfect!
>
> The hotel is in a convenient location. It's at 2345 Golden Gate Ave. There's a subway stop a block away and a bus stop. There are a lot of shops and restaurants nearby. The San Francisco Museum of Modern Art is on Second St., a few blocks from there, too.
>
> The hotel has free parking. It has a business center and three large meeting rooms. There's a pool, a sauna, and a really good fitness center. There's a gift shop and a nice café on the first floor.
>
> Let me know if you want more information!
>
> Yusef

B Read the Reading Skill. Then read the email again. Take notes about the Grand Hotel.

Hotel location and places nearby	What the hotel has
convenient location	free parking

READING SKILL Take notes

As you read, write a few words about important details. Don't write complete sentences.

3 MAKE IT PERSONAL

Look for hotels in San Francisco. Find one that is good for a vacation. 🔍

A Do you like the Grand Hotel? Why or why not?

B PAIRS Compare your answers in 3A. Do you want the same things in a hotel?

□ I CAN READ ABOUT A HOTEL.

WRITE ABOUT A HOTEL

1 FOCUS ON WRITING

A Read the Writing Skill.

B Read the email on page 82 again.
Circle the abbreviations for *Street* and *Avenue*.

> **WRITING SKILL** Abbreviations
>
> When writing an address, you can abbreviate words in the street name. For example, abbreviate the word *Road* like this:
> *234 River* **Rd.**

2 PLAN YOUR WRITING

A Think about a hotel. Complete the chart with information about the hotel.

Name of hotel:	
Address:	

Places and services in the hotel	Places and services around the hotel

B PAIRS Talk about the hotel. Describe where it is and the services it has.

This hotel has ...   Nearby there is ...

3 WRITE

Write an email about a hotel you know. Tell where it is. Describe its places and services. Describe what's in the neighborhood. Use the email on page 82 as a model.

4 REVISE YOUR WRITING

A PAIRS Read your partner's email. Complete the chart.

Did your partner ...?	Yes	No
use abbreviations in addresses		
describe the places and services in the hotel		
describe the neighborhood		

B PAIRS Can you improve your partner's email? Make suggestions. Then revise your writing.

5 PROOFREAD

Read your email again. Check your spelling, punctuation, and capitalization.

☐ I CAN WRITE ABOUT A HOTEL.

PUT IT TOGETHER

1 MEDIA PROJECT

A ▶08-19 **Listen or watch. Answer the questions.**

1. What are Ahmet's favorite places?

   _____

   _____

2. Where does he meet his friends?

   _____

B **Show your own photos.**

Step 1 Think about your neighborhood or a neighborhood near your school. Take 4-6 photos of some of the places.

Step 2 Show the photos to the class. Talk about the neighborhood.

Step 3 Answer questions from the class about the neighborhood. Get feedback on your presentation.

2 LEARNING STRATEGY

> **PRACTICE THE PRONUNCIATION**
> Identify sounds that you find difficult. Look for ways to practice the pronunciations. Use online recordings to listen and repeat.

toothpaste

Review the vocabulary in the unit. Which words are difficult to pronounce? Listen to those words in your app. Listen and repeat.

3 REFLECT AND PLAN

A Look back through the unit. Check the things you learned. Highlight the things you need to learn.

Speaking objectives
- [ ] Ask for personal care items
- [ ] Give directions in a building
- [ ] Talk about where places are located

Vocabulary
- [ ] Personal care items
- [ ] Places in a hotel
- [ ] Places in a city

Pronunciation
- [ ] The sound /ʃ/
- [ ] Main stress

Grammar
- [ ] *There is / There are*
- [ ] *Like, want, need +* infinitives
- [ ] Prepositions of place: *At, on, in*

Reading
- [ ] Take notes

Writing
- [ ] Abbreviations

B What will you do to learn the things you highlighted? For example, use your App, review your Student Book, or do other practice. Make a plan.

‹ Notes	Done
Review the grammar chart in lesson 3, page 80.	

9 IS EVERYTHING OK?

LEARNING GOALS

In this unit, you
⊘ describe things people own
⊘ talk about what you're doing
⊘ talk about daily activities
⊘ read and write about computer problems

GET STARTED

A Read the unit title and learning goals.

B Look at the photo of an office. What do you see?

C Now read Dan's message. What kind of day is it?

DAN LU
@DanL

Back in NYC for a few days. Not a good start to the day; I'm already late.

DAN LU

@DanL

I'm not ready for my meeting with Gaby! 😫

 1 VOCABULARY Describing things

A ▶09-01 Listen. Then listen and repeat.

| old | new | fast | slow | heavy | light |

| noisy | quiet | hard | soft | small | big |

B Label the pictures. Use words from 1A.

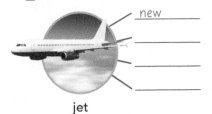

new _____

jet

kitten

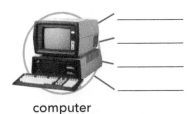

computer

C PAIRS Compare answers.

I think the kitten is soft ...

2 GRAMMAR Possessive nouns; *This / that / these / those*

' is called an apostrophe

Possessive nouns

Singular	Plural	Irregular plural
the teacher**'s** book	the teacher**s'** books	men**'s** clothing
the boy**'s** bike	the boy**s'** bikes	women**'s** clothing
Jane**'s** desk	the Smith**s'** house	children**'s** clothing
Add **'s** after the noun.	Add **'** after the final **s**.	Add **'s** after the noun.

This / That / These / Those

Singular		Plural	
this book	**that book**	**these pens**	**those pens**

>> FOR PRACTICE, GO TO PAGE 124

3 PRONUNCIATION

A ▶09-03 Listen. Notice the main stress. Then listen and repeat.

> A: There's no **chair** in the office.   A: **This** chair?
>
> B: Take **Mike's** chair.   B: No, that's **my** chair.

> **Moving the main stress**
>
> At the beginning of a conversation, the main stress is often on the last important word. After that, we move the main stress to highlight new or different information.

B ▶09-04 Listen. Underline the main stress. Then listen and repeat.

1. A: Is that your new <u>phone</u>?   2. A: This chair is really hard.   3. A: I need a quiet office.
   B: No, this is my old phone.   B: Here, use my chair.   B: You can use that office.

C PAIRS Practice the conversations in 3B.

4 CONVERSATION

A ▶09-05 Listen or watch. Circle the correct answer.

1. Where is Ester?
   a. She's in the ladies' room.
   b. She's out to lunch.
   c. Tina doesn't know.
2. Dan has a ___ with Gaby.
   a. video call   b. phone call   c. meeting
3. At the end of the video, ___ .
   a. Dan isn't ready for the meeting
   b. everything is great
   c. Dan needs a notepad

B ▶09-06 Read the Conversation Skill. Listen or watch. Complete the conversation.

> Tina: Is everything OK?
>
> Dan: It's really noisy here. Is there another desk I can use?
>
> Tina: You can use _____ . It's really quiet there.
>
> Dan: Can I use _____ chair?
>
> Tina: Sure. Are you all right now?
>
> Dan: Yeah, it's just my computer. It's very _____ .

> **CONVERSATION SKILL**
> **Ask about a problem**
>
> To ask about a problem, say:
> • *Is everything OK?*
> • *What's wrong?*
> Listen or watch the conversation in 4A. Raise your hand when you hear someone ask about a problem.

C ▶09-07 Listen and repeat. Then practice with a partner.

5 TRY IT YOURSELF

A MAKE IT PERSONAL Choose three things you own, for example: clothing, technology, or furniture. Write descriptive adjectives for each one.

B PAIRS Compare your descriptions.
A: Do you have something old?
B: Yes, I have an old cell phone. It's small and light, but it's old and slow.

☐ I CAN DESCRIBE THINGS PEOPLE OWN.

DAN LU
@DanL

NOW I'm having problems with the video call. 😠

1 VOCABULARY Technology

A ▶09-08 Listen. Then listen and repeat.

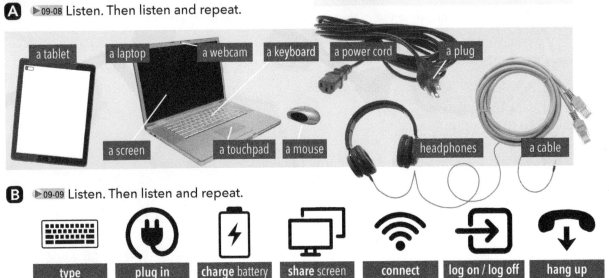

a tablet   a laptop   a webcam   a keyboard   a power cord   a plug

a screen   a touchpad   a mouse   headphones   a cable

B ▶09-09 Listen. Then listen and repeat.

| type | plug in | charge battery | share screen | connect | log on / log off | hang up |

C PAIRS Make pairs of words that go together. Explain why.

A: *Plug in goes with power cord.*
B: Right, you plug in the end of the cord.

2 GRAMMAR Present continuous: Statements and questions

COACH

Affirmative statements			Negative statements			
Subject	*Be*	**Verb + -ing**	**Subject**	*Be*	**Not**	**Verb + -ing**
I	am		I	'm		
We They	are	talking.	We They	're	not	talking.
He	is		He	's		

Yes/no questions			Short answers	
Be	**Subject**	**Verb + -ing**	**Affirmative**	**Negative**
Are	you		Yes, I **am**.	No, I'**m not**.
Are	they	working?	Yes, they **are**.	No, they **aren't**. / No, they'**re not**.
Is	he		Yes, he **is**.	No, he **isn't**. / No, he'**s not**.

Wh- questions				Answers
Wh- word	*Be*	**Subject**	**Verb + -ing**	
What	are	you	**doing**?	I'm fixing the computer.
Where	is	he	**going**?	He's going to work.
Who	are	you	**talking** to?	I'm talking to Jen.
Why		they	**running**?	Because they are late.

>> FOR PRACTICE, GO TO PAGE 125

3 PRONUNCIATION

COACH

A ▶09-11 Listen. Notice the intonation. Then listen and repeat.

What are you **doing**?   Who are you **talking** to?

Are you **working**?   Are you talking to **Gaby**?

Intonation in questions

Intonation usually goes up ↗ at the end of *yes/no* questions. Intonation usually goes down ↘ at the end of *wh-* questions.

B ▶09-12 Listen. Does the intonation go up ↗ or down ↘ at the end? Circle ↗ or ↘. Then listen and repeat.

1. Are you hanging up? ↗ ↘
2. Are you logging on? ↗ ↘
3. Is it charging? ↗ ↘
4. How is he doing? ↗ ↘
5. Where are you going? ↗ ↘
6. What is she typing? ↗ ↘

C PAIRS Practice the questions in 3B. Then write two more questions.

4 CONVERSATION

A ▶09-13 Listen or watch. Check the true statements.

- ☐ Dan can't hear Gaby.
- ☐ Gaby can't see Dan.
- ☐ Gaby calls Dan on her tablet.
- ☐ Dan gets a new laptop.
- ☐ Dan wants to share his screen.
- ☐ Gaby doesn't have a power cord.

B ▶09-14 Listen or watch. Complete the conversation.

Dan: What _____?

Gaby: _____ you on my tablet.

Dan: OK … Nope. It _____ .

Gaby: How about *your* computer?

Dan: Let me check. The webcam isn't working.

C ▶09-15 Listen and repeat. Then practice with a partner.

D PAIRS Make new conversations. Use these words or your own ideas.

laptop   keyboard

5 TRY IT YOURSELF

A GROUPS On separate pieces of paper, write 8-10 activities you can do with technology. Fold each paper. Give your folded papers to another group.

use a mouse   type

B GROUPS Play charades. Student A, choose one paper. Don't show it to your group. Act out the activity. Group members, guess the activity. You have three guesses. Keep score!

■ I CAN TALK ABOUT WHAT I'M DOING.

LESSON 3 TALK ABOUT DAILY ACTIVITIES

DAN LU
@DanL

Check out this podcast—Carly's
Corner—it has some good advice.

1 VOCABULARY Daily activities

A ▶09-16 **Listen. Then listen and repeat.**

get up

brush your teeth

take a shower

get dressed

6:00 A.M.
eat breakfast

12:00 P.M.
eat lunch

7:00 P.M.
eat dinner

leave the house

get home

go online

relax

go to bed

B ▶09-17 **Listen. Then write the activity.**

1. _go online_
2. _____
3. _____
4. _____
5. _____
6. _____

C PAIRS **Compare your answers.**

2 GRAMMAR Adverbs of frequency

				Notes
100%		always		• The adverb of frequency goes before the action verb.
		usually		*He **always** gets up at 6:00 A.M.*
		often		
50%	I		eat breakfast.	• The adverb of frequency goes after the verb *be*.
		sometimes		*He's **never** late. He's **always** on time.*
		rarely		• Use *how often* to ask about frequency.
0%		never		***How often** do you go online?*

>> FOR PRACTICE, GO TO PAGE 126

3 LISTENING

A ▶09-19 Listen to the podcast. This podcast is about ___ .
   a. different kinds of exercise
   b. ideas to help you sleep at night
   c. ways to feel more relaxed

> **LISTENING SKILL**
> **Listen for numbering**
>
> Listen for number words like *first, second, third,* and *fourth.* Speakers often use these words to organize their ideas.

B ▶09-19 Read the Listening Skill. Listen again. Number the pictures. Then complete the tips.

Sleep for _____ a night.

Always _____ .

Drink _8 glasses of water_ a day.

Always _____ at the same time.

1

_____ every day.

C PAIRS Which tip do you think is the most important? I think exercise is the most important.

4 TRY IT YOURSELF

A MAKE IT PERSONAL Which things in 3B do you always / sometimes / never do?
   A: I always sleep for 7 or 8 hours.   **B:** Not me. I sometimes only sleep 4 or 5 hours.

B TAKE A POLL Interview three classmates. Complete the chart.
Write their answers to the questions.

Name:			
1. What time do you usually go to bed?			
2. What time do you usually get up?			
3. Do you always eat breakfast?			
4. Do you exercise often?			
5. How many glasses of water do you drink a day?			
6. Are you ever stressed out?			

C CLASS Report to the class.

■ I CAN **TALK ABOUT DAILY ACTIVITIES.**

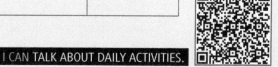

LESSON 4   READ ABOUT COMPUTER PROBLEMS

DAN LU

@DanL

I need lots of help with my laptop.

1 BEFORE YOU READ

Do you ever have problems with your computer?
What kind of problems?

2 READ

A ▶09-20 Listen. Read the email. Why does Dan need Greg's help? _____

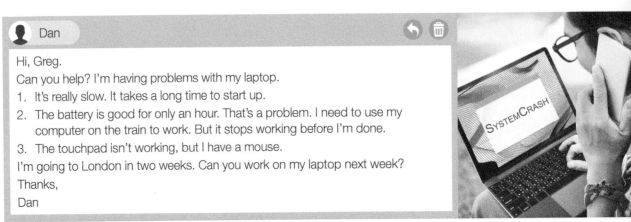

Dan

Hi, Greg.
Can you help? I'm having problems with my laptop.
1. It's really slow. It takes a long time to start up.
2. The battery is good for only an hour. That's a problem. I need to use my computer on the train to work. But it stops working before I'm done.
3. The touchpad isn't working, but I have a mouse.
I'm going to London in two weeks. Can you work on my laptop next week?
Thanks,
Dan

B Read the email again. Check (✓) the problems Dan has with his laptop.

- ☐ It is too heavy.
- ☐ It is too noisy.
- ✓ It is too slow.
- ☐ The touchpad doesn't work well.
- ☐ The battery is bad.
- ☐ The keyboard is broken.

C Read the Reading Skill. Then read the email again. Make inferences. Circle the best answers.

1. How long does it take Dan's laptop to start?
   a. 3 seconds   b. more than two minutes
2. How long is Dan's commute to work?
   a. less than an hour   b. more than an hour
3. Dan doesn't need his touchpad fixed because ___.
   a. he uses the mouse   b. it isn't broken
4. When does Dan need his computer?
   a. in one week   b. in two weeks

> **READING SKILL Make inferences**
>
> Sometimes writers do not state all of their ideas in the text. While you read, use information from the text and / or pictures to figure out ideas that are not stated.

3 MAKE IT PERSONAL

A What kind of computer do you use at home and at work? What do you like about it? What do you not like?

B PAIRS Discuss the computers you use and what you like or dislike about them.

The webcam on my laptop ...

> Find out the history of the first cell phone? 🔍

▢ I CAN READ ABOUT COMPUTER PROBLEMS.

WRITE ABOUT COMPUTER PROBLEMS

1 FOCUS ON WRITING

A Read the Writing Skill.

B Read the email on page 92 again.
Circle the numbers in a list.

> **WRITING SKILL** **Write a list**
>
> In business emails, you can
> write a list. This makes your
> writing easy to read. Use
> numbers or bullet points (•).

2 PLAN YOUR WRITING

A Imagine you have problems with your laptop, computer, tablet, or phone. Look at the
technology words on page 88. Complete the chart.

Item: _____

Problem:	Problem:	Problem:
_____	_____	_____
Explanation / Example:	Explanation / Example:	Explanation / Example:
_____	_____	_____

B PAIRS Talk about your technology problems.

My keyboard is …

3 WRITE

Write an email about problems with technology. Describe the problems.
Make a list of the problems. Ask for help. Use the email on page 92 as a model.

4 REVISE YOUR WRITING

A PAIRS Read your partner's email. Complete the chart.

Did your partner …?	Yes	No
describe the problems		
ask for help		
write a list with numbers or bullet points		

B PAIRS Can you improve your partner's email? Make suggestions. Then revise your writing.

5 PROOFREAD

Read your email again. Check your spelling,
punctuation, and capitalization.

☐ I CAN WRITE ABOUT COMPUTER PROBLEMS.

PUT IT TOGETHER

1 MEDIA PROJECT

A ▶09-21 Listen or watch. Check (✓) the activity each person is doing.

	Karin	Hana	Mio	Ren & Yuna
taking photos				
playing video games				
texting friends				
checking email				

B Show your own photos.

Step 1 Think about technology. Take 4–6 photos of your friends or family members on their phones, computers, or other devices.

Step 2 Show the photos to the class. Talk about each one and explain what each person is doing.

Step 3 Answer questions about the photos. Get feedback on your presentation.

2 LEARNING STRATEGY

> **WRITE THE RULE**
> To understand grammar, find examples of a grammar structure and write the rule.

Make a list of phrases or sentences from the grammar charts in this unit. Write a grammar rule in your own words.

the teacher's book
the boy's bike
Jane's desk

Rule: To form the possessive of
regular singular nouns, add 's

3 REFLECT AND PLAN

A Look back through the unit. Check the things you learned. Highlight the things you need to learn.

Speaking objectives
- [ ] Describe things people own
- [ ] Talk about what I'm doing
- [ ] Talk about daily activities

Vocabulary
- [ ] Describing things
- [ ] Technology
- [ ] Daily activities

Pronunciation
- [ ] Moving the main stress
- [ ] Intonation in questions

Grammar
- [ ] Possessive nouns
- [ ] *This / that / these / those*
- [ ] Present continuous: Statements and questions
- [ ] Adverbs of frequency

Reading
- [ ] Make inferences

Writing
- [ ] Write a list

B What will you do to learn the things you highlighted? For example, use your App, review your Student Book, or do other practice. Make a plan.

> ‹ Notes   Done
>
> Do the Learning Strategy:
> Write the rule, page 94.

10 HOW WAS YOUR WEEKEND?

LEARNING GOALS

In this unit, you
- ⊘ describe your weekend
- ⊘ talk about past activities
- ⊘ talk about a past vacation
- ⊘ read and write about a vacation

GET STARTED

A Read the unit title and learning goals.

B Look at the photo. What do you see?

C Now read Tina's message. What kind of weekend did she have?

TINA ADAMS
@TinaA

I'm back at work after a great weekend.

TINA ADAMS
@TinaA

What a perfect weekend! Can't wait to show everyone the photos.

 1 VOCABULARY Describing activities

A ▶10-01 **Listen. Then listen and repeat.**

crowded · empty · fun · boring · relaxing · stressful

clean · dirty · easy · difficult

B Write five places and/or activities. Use one word from 1A to describe each one.

New York = crowded
football = fun

C PAIRS Student A, say one of your places or activities from 1B. Student B, guess the description. Keep score.

2 GRAMMAR Simple past with *be*

Affirmative statements			Negative statements			
Subject	***Be***		**Subject**	***Be***	**Not**	
I			I			
She	was		She	was		
We		happy.	We		not	sad.
They	were		They	were		
You			You			

Note: Use contractions in speaking and informal writing.

was + not = wasn't
were + not = weren't

Yes/no questions			Short answers						
Be	**Subject**		**Affirmative**			**Negative**			
Was	I		Yes,	I	was.	No,	I	wasn't.	
	he	wrong?		he			he		
Were	we			we	were.		we	weren't.	
	they			they			they		

Wh- questions				Answers
Wh- word	Be	Subject		
Who	was		at the party?	Kyle **was** at the party.
What		the problem?		The test **was** difficult.
Where	was	your hotel?		It **was** on Summit Avenue.
When	were	you	in Brazil?	I **was** in Brazil in 1999.
Why		they	late?	Because there **was** traffic.
How	was	your vacation?		It **was** relaxing.

>> FOR PRACTICE, GO TO PAGE 127

3 CONSERVATION

A ▶10-03 **Listen or watch. Read the sentences. Write *T* for *True* and *F* for *False*.**

___ 1. Cole was at the beach.
___ 2. It's warm and sunny at the beach.
___ 3. Tina was at the beach.

___ 4. The beach was crowded.
___ 5. Tina likes to swim at the beach.
___ 6. Tina likes to sit in the sun.

B ▶10-04 **Listen or watch. Complete the conversation.**

Cole: _____ your weekend?

Tina: It was wonderful! I was at the beach.

Cole: Really? Lucky you.

Tina: Yeah, it was beautiful but crowded. There were a lot of tourists.

Cole: How was the weather?

Tina: Perfect. It was warm and sunny.

Cole: It sounds like _____ really relaxing.

C ▶10-05 **Listen and repeat. Then practice with a partner.**

4 TRY IT YOURSELF

A MAKE IT PERSONAL **Talk about your weekend.**
A: How was your weekend?   B: It wasn't very good. I was home all weekend.

B WALK AROUND **Talk to three classmates about their weekends. Complete the chart.**

Name	Place	Description

C CLASS **Tell the class about someone's weekend.**
Oscar's weekend was boring. He was at work. It was stressful.

☐ I CAN DESCRIBE MY WEEKEND.

TINA ADAMS
@TinaA

Our usual Monday morning—talking about our weekends—wishing it was Friday.

1 VOCABULARY Weekend activities

A ▶10-06 Listen. Then listen and repeat.

stay home

clean the house

wash the car

work in the yard

visit friends

text a friend

talk to a friend

watch movies on TV

go dancing

play tennis

B Circle the activities in 1A that you like to do.

C PAIRS Compare. Do you like to do the same activities?
A: I like to talk on the phone. B: I don't. I always text.

2 GRAMMAR Simple past: Statements and *yes/no* questions

Affirmative statements

Subject	Verb	
I You He She We They	cleaned	the kitchen.

Negative statements

Subject	*Did*	*Not*	Verb	
I You He She We They	did	not	clean	the living room.

Note: Use contractions in speaking and informal writing.
did + not = didn't

Yes/no questions

Did	Subject	Verb
Did	he you they	help?

Short answers

Affirmative			Negative		
Yes,	he I they	did.	No,	he I they	didn't.

Notes
- To form the simple past, use base form of the verb + **-ed**: clean**ed**.
- For verbs that end in **e**, use base form + **d**: danc**ed**.
- Use the base form of the verb with *did / didn't*: I didn't walk to school.

>> FOR PRACTICE, GO TO PAGE 128

3 PRONUNCIATION

COACH

A 10-08 **Listen. Notice the pronunciation of *-ed*. Then listen and repeat the past tense verbs.**

no extra syllable	extra syllable /ɪd/
wash → washed	text → texted
talk → talked	need → needed

The simple past *-ed* ending

We pronounce the simple past *-ed* as an extra syllable /ɪd/ only after the sound /t/ or /d/. After other sounds, the *e* in *-ed* is silent.

B 10-09 **Listen. Circle the past tense verbs that have an extra syllable. Then listen and repeat.**

1. played 2. watched 3. visited 4. worked 5. started 6. danced 7. stayed

C PAIRS **Student A, say an activity from 1A. Student B, say the activity in the simple past.**

A: Clean the house. B: Cleaned the house.

4 CONVERSATION

A 10-10 **Listen or watch. Circle the correct answer.**

1. Cole's weekend was *stressful / fine / boring*.
2. On Saturday night, Cole *stayed home / cleaned the house / went to a club*.
3. Cole and his friends *waited / went to a movie / danced for hours*.
4. Tina thinks Cole's weekend was *boring / stressful /exciting*.

B 10-11 **Read the Conversation Skill. Listen or watch. Complete the conversation.**

Tina: ________________ anything fun this weekend?

Cole: Not really. I just ________________ . I did some work around the house.

Tina: That's too bad.

Cole: No, it was good, actually. I washed the car, and I ____________ the garage.

Tina: Well, sometimes that kind of work is relaxing.

Cole: I think so, too.

CONVERSATION SKILL
Agree with someone

To show that you have the same opinion and agree with someone, say:

- *I think so, too.*
- *I agree.*

Listen or watch the conversation in 4A. Raise your hand when you hear someone agree.

C 10-12 **Listen and repeat. Then practice with a partner.**

5 TRY IT YOURSELF

MAKE IT PERSONAL **Student A, ask a *yes/no* question about last weekend. Student B, give a short answer and add another sentence.**

A: Did you clean the house last weekend?
B: No, I didn't. I worked in the yard. Did you go dancing?

☐ I CAN TALK ABOUT PAST ACTIVITIES.

TINA ADAMS
@TinaA

Just heard an interesting podcast about a vacation that changed someone's life.

1 VOCABULARY Vacation activities

A ▶10-13 **Listen. Then listen and repeat.**

take a tour

take a boat ride

take a ride

take a train trip

fly

go swimming

go shopping

go sightseeing

meet new people

eat out

B ▶10-14 **Listen and number the activities.**

___ take a tour	___ go shopping	___ take a boat ride	_1_ fly
___ take a train trip	___ go swimming	___ meet new people	___ eat out

C GROUPS Act out one of the activities in 1A. The first person to guess correctly acts out a different activity.

2 GRAMMAR Simple past: *Wh-* questions and irregular verbs

COACH

Wh- questions			Answers	Irregular verbs			
Wh- word	**Did**			**Base form of verb**	**Past**	**Base form of verb**	**Past**
Who		she **see**?	She **saw** Melissa.	become	became	go	went
What		you **buy**?	I **bought** a gift.	bring	brought	have	had
Where		they **go**?	They **went** to China.	buy	bought	know	knew
When	did	we **meet**?	We **met** in 2015.	come	came	make	made
Why		you **fly**?	I **flew** to get home today.	eat	ate	meet	met
				fall	fell	ride	rode
How		you **get** here?	I **got** here by bus.	fly	flew	see	saw
				get	got	swim	swam
				give	gave	take	took

>> FOR PRACTICE, GO TO PAGE 129

▶ 3 PRONUNCIATION

COACH

A ▶10-16 Listen. Notice the blended pronunciation of *did you*. Then listen and repeat.

Blending *did you*

In questions with *did you*, we often blend *did* and *you* together. We pronounce *did* and *you* together as "didja" /dɪdʒə/.

/dɪdʒə/   /dɪdʒə/   /dɪdʒə/

Where did_you go?   What did_you do there?   Did_you do anything fun?

B ▶10-17 Listen. Write *do you* or *did you*. Then listen and repeat.

1. _____ walk to school?
2. _____ text your friends on Saturday?
3. What _____ do on the weekend?
4. Where _____ go on vacation?

C PAIRS Ask and answer the questions in 3B.

4 LISTENING

A ▶10-18 Listen to the radio show. Trudy describes this vacation because her parents ___.

a. met in Europe   b. went on vacation alone   c. met her husband's parents

B ▶10-18 Listen again. Read the sentences. Write *T* for True and *F* for False.

_F_ 1. Trudy and her husband took a tour of Europe.
___ 2. Trudy's parents met Don and Cindy in Europe.
___ 3. Don and Cindy came to visit Trudy's family.
___ 4. Trudy and her brother saw Don and Cindy every summer.
___ 5. Trudy met Mark when she was 18 years old.

C ▶10-18 Read the Listening Skill. Listen. Make inferences to answer the questions. Explain your answers.

1. Why did Cindy give Trudy's mom her address?

   _____
   _____

2. Did the families live near each other?

   _____
   _____

LISTENING SKILL Make inferences

People don't always say everything they are thinking. Use your experience and your knowledge to figure out, or make an inference, about what is probably true.

5 TRY IT YOURSELF

A MAKE IT PERSONAL Think about a great vacation. Use real or imaginary information. Take notes.
Who? What? Where? When? How?

B PAIRS Prepare a radio show. Interview your partner about his or her great vacation. Take notes.

C CLASS Do a live interview for the class.

■ I CAN TALK ABOUT A PAST VACATION.

TINA ADAMS
@TinaA

Finally showing photos of my vacation. You won't believe the views.

1 BEFORE YOU READ

When was the last time you had a vacation?
Where did you go?

2 READ

A ▶10-19 Listen. Read Tina's post. What does she talk about? _____

Tina Adams shared **3 photos**   3 hrs ago

My vacation was great. Last week I went to Tulum, Mexico, with my friend Anita. We stayed in a hotel near the beach. Our room was big and sunny. We had a view of the water from our balcony.

On our first day, we had breakfast in the hotel. Then we took a tour of the beautiful town. We had a wonderful lunch and then went shopping. In the evening, we had dinner and danced all night at a club.

The next few days, we went to the beach. We went swimming, sat in the sun, and relaxed. One day we took a boat ride. Every night we went out for dinner. The food was terrific. We had a great time and I took lots of photos!

B Read the post again. Write 5-8 *wh*-questions. Use *who*, *what*, *where*, *when*, and *how*.

C PAIRS Answer the questions you wrote in 2B.

D Read the Reading Skill. Circle the main idea of Tina's post.

   a. Tina went to Tulum, Mexico, on vacation.

   b. Tina had a great vacation.

   c. Tina took lots of photos on her vacation.

> **READING SKILL Main Idea**
>
> The main idea is the most important idea in a text.

3 MAKE IT PERSONAL

> Find a place for a great vacation. 🔍

A Think about what you like to do on vacation. Take notes.

B PAIRS Discuss what you like to do on vacation. Do you like the same things?

■ I CAN READ ABOUT A VACATION.

1 FOCUS ON WRITING

A Read the Writing Skill.

B Read Tina's post on page 102 again. Circle the commas.

> **WRITING SKILL Commas**
>
> Use commas:
> - Between a time expression and the rest of the sentence
> - Between the name of a city and country (If this is in the middle of a sentence, use a comma after the country too.)
> - After each item in a list of three or more items

2 PLAN YOUR WRITING

A Think of a vacation. Take notes in the chart.

When?	Where?
Who?	**What?**

B PAIRS Talk about your vacation. Describe when, where, what you did, and who you went with. What is the main idea?

I went to …   I went with …

3 WRITE

Write a post about a vacation you took. Describe when and where you went, who you went with, what you did, and how you liked it. Use the post on page 102 as a model.

4 REVISE YOUR WRITING

A PAIRS Read your partner's post. Complete the chart.

Did your partner …?	Yes	No
write a main idea		
give details		
use commas correctly		

B PAIRS Can you improve your partner's post? Make suggestions. Then revise your writing.

5 PROOFREAD

Read your post again. Check your spelling, punctuation, and capitalization.

■ I CAN WRITE ABOUT A VACATION.

PUT IT TOGETHER

1 MEDIA PROJECT

A ▶10-20 Listen or watch. Complete the chart with Daniel's activities.

Morning	Afternoon	Evening

B Show your own photos.

Step 1 Think about a weekend or vacation in the past. Choose 4–6 photos or take new photos of what you do on the weekend.

Step 2 Show the photos to the class. Talk about what you did.

Step 3 Answer questions about the photos. Get feedback on your presentation.

2 LEARNING STRATEGY

> **WRITE SENTENCES**
> Write sentences to practice using irregular verbs. Choose verbs that are difficult for you. Write sentences with them. This helps you learn how to use the verbs.

Review the verbs in the unit. Write sentences about what you did in the past.

I bought a book yesterday. I took a vacation at the beach last year.

3 REFLECT AND PLAN

A Look back through the unit. Check the things you learned. Highlight the things you need to learn.

Speaking objectives
- [ ] Describe my weekend
- [ ] Talk about past activities
- [ ] Talk about a past vacation

Vocabulary
- [ ] Describing activities
- [ ] Weekend activities
- [ ] Vacation activities

Pronunciation
- [ ] The simple past -ed ending
- [ ] Blending did you

Grammar
- [ ] Simple past with be
- [ ] Simple past: Statements and yes/no questions
- [ ] Simple past: Wh- questions
- [ ] Irregular verbs

Reading
- [ ] Main Idea

Writing
- [ ] Commas

B What will you do to learn the things you highlighted? For example, use your App, review your Student Book, or do other practice. Make a plan.

‹ Notes   Done

In the app, do the Lesson 1 listening practice: Talk about a past vacation

A Write *a* or *an*.

1. _a_ teacher
2. ___ dentist
3. ___ manager
4. ___ architect
5. ___ flight attendant
6. ___ illustrator
7. ___ chef
8. ___ doctor
9. ___ engineer
10. ___ accountant
11. ___ scientist
12. ___ programmer

B Complete the sentences. Use the correct form of *be*. Use contractions when possible.

MEET MY TEAM AT A&H DESIGN!

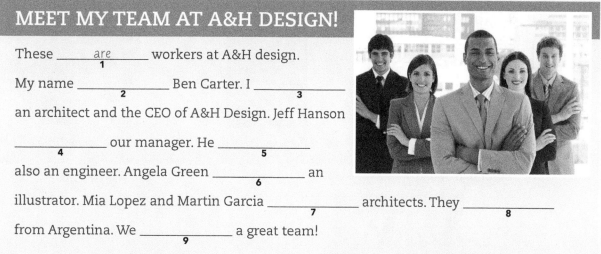

These ____are____ workers at A&H design.
1

My name _____ Ben Carter. I _____
2   3

an architect and the CEO of A&H Design. Jeff Hanson

_____ our manager. He _____
4   5

also an engineer. Angela Green _____ an
6

illustrator. Mia Lopez and Martin Garcia _____ architects. They _____
7   8

from Argentina. We _____ a great team!
9

C ▶01-10 Listen. Complete the sentences.

1. _____You're_____ good doctors.
2. _____ Dennis Andrews.
3. _____ managers.
4. _____ teachers.
5. _____ nice name.
6. _____ engineer.
7. _____ illustrator.
8. _____ accountant.

A ▶01-17 Listen to the sentences. Are the nouns singular or plural? Check (✓) the correct box.

	1	2	3	4	5	6	7	8
Singular								
Plural	✓							

B Complete the sentences. Use the correct form of *have* or *need*.

Luca and I _____*have*_____ a small office. It _____ two windows. We
      1 (have)   **2 (have)**

_____ large desks. I _____ a new chair. Luca _____ a phone.
3 (have)   **4 (need)**   **5 (need)**

We _____ good computers. Luca _____ papers on his desk. He
    6 (have)   **7 (have)**

_____ a file cabinet. We _____ a bigger office!
8 (need)   **9 (need)**

C Look at the pictures. Complete the sentences. Use the correct form of the noun.

1. We have twenty
   _____*pens*_____ .

2. The store has five
   different _____ .

3. The teacher has four
   _____ .

4. We need five
   _____
   for the meeting.

5. The bookcase has
   six _____ .

6. We have three
   _____ in the
   classroom.

7. Eric and Rita need two
   _____ .

8. They have two _____
   in the office.

A ▶02-02 Listen to the sentences. Check (✓) the possessive adjectives you hear.

1. ☐ her   ✓ my   4. ☐ our   ☐ your   7. ☐ your   ☐ our
2. ☐ our   ☐ her   5. ☐ her   ☐ his   8. ☐ her   ☐ your
3. ☐ their ☐ our   6. ☐ their ☐ our   9. ☐ his   ☐ their

B Look at the picture. Complete the conversation. Write the correct possessive adjective.

A: Here's a picture of _____my_____ family.
   ₁

B: Who's that?

A: That's _____ brother.
              ₂

B: What's _____ name?
              ₃

A: _____ name is Andrew.
     ₄

B: And who's that?

A: That's _____ wife.
              ₅

   _____ name is Dora.
   ₆
   And that's _____ son.
                  ₇

B: What's _____ name?
              ₈

A: Nathan.

Ted   Nathan   Dora   Olivia   Andrew

B: These are _____ parents?
                  ₉

A: Yes, _____ names are Ted
           ₁₀
   and Olivia.

B: Where are you?

A: I'm behind the camera!

C Complete the sentences. Write the correct possessive adjective.

1. That is Robert. Stephan is
   _____his_____ grandson.

2. I'm Emily. Stephan is
   _____ son.

3. That's Maria. John is
   _____ father.

4. That's Tim. Carol is
   _____ daughter.

5. That's Anna. Will is
   _____ grandson.

6. That's Will, and this is Carol.
   Lisa and Tim are
   _____ parents.

7. That's Carol. Robert is
   _____ grandfather.

8. That's Stephan. John is
   _____ father.

9. That's Lisa. Tim is
   _____ husband.

Robert   Anna

Lisa   Tim   Emily   John

Will   Carol   Maria   Stephan

A ▶02-10 Listen to the sentences. Are the sentences affirmative or negative? Check (✓) the correct box.

	1	2	3	4	5	6	7	8
Affirmative	✓							
Negative								

B Read Samantha's online profile. Change the false sentences from affirmative to negative. Then write true sentences. Use contractions when possible.

Samantha Rivers

Relationship Status:
married to Brian Rivers
Age: 42
Home: Boston

About me:
I'm a designer, a wife, and a mother of two
great girls, Lara and Maddie. They're in
high school.
My life is busy, but it's good!

1. Samantha is a programmer. _____Samantha isn't a programmer. She's a designer._____
2. She is 32 years old. _____
3. She is single. _____
4. Brian is her son. _____
5. Her home is in Portland. _____
6. Lara and Maddie are her friends. _____
7. Her daughters are lawyers. _____

C Write a *yes/no* question for each prompt. Then complete the short answer. Use contractions when possible.

1. she / single
   A: _____Is she single?_____
   B: _____No, she's not._____

2. you and Carl / friends
   A: _____
   B: Yes, _____ .

3. Meg / married
   A: _____
   B: No, _____ .

4. Dana and Adam / your kids
   A: _____
   B: Yes, _____ .

5. I / late
   A: _____
   B: Yes, _____ .

6. Rob / your brother
   A: _____
   B: No, _____ .

7. you / Mike
   A: _____
   B: Yes, _____ .

8. they / co-workers
   A: _____
   B: No, _____ .

9. Richard / her boyfriend
   A: _____
   B: No, _____ .

10. we / friends
    A: _____
    B: Yes, _____ .

A ▶02-15 Listen to the sentences. Check (✓) the form of the verb you hear.

1. ✓ live   ☐ lives   5. ☐ work   ☐ works
2. ☐ live   ☐ lives   6. ☐ live   ☐ lives
3. ☐ work   ☐ works   7. ☐ work   ☐ works
4. ☐ live   ☐ lives   8. ☐ work   ☐ works

B Complete the paragraph. Use the correct form of the verbs in parentheses.

My brother Max _____lives_____ in South Korea with his family. His wife Barb _____
1 (live)   **2 (work)**
for a technology company. Max _____ at Seoul National University. He's an English
                              3 (work)
professor. Max and Barb _____ three children. Their daughters _____
                        4 (have)   **5 (live)**
in Seoul, not far from their parents. They both _____ at a hospital. Their son
                                                6 (work)
_____ in the United States. He's 22, and he _____ for a computer
7 (live)   **8 (work)**
company in California. He _____ a great job as a programmer.
                         9 (have)

C Complete the paragraph. Use the correct form of *live*, *work*, *have*, and *need*.

● Bogota
Colombia
●
Cali

José now _____lives_____ and _____ in Bogota, Colombia, but he's from Cali. All
            1   **2**
his family still _____ in Cali. His two sisters _____ in a beautiful apartment
                3   **4**
in the city center. They both _____ for Diaz Design Company. José's brother
                              5
also _____ and works in Cali. He's a doctor. He's married and he and his wife
     6
_____ a baby boy. They _____ in a small apartment. They _____
7   **8**   **9**
a big apartment.

UNIT 3, LESSON 1   ADJECTIVE + NOUN PLACEMENT

A ▶03-03 **Listen to the conversation. Complete the sentences.**

A: Hey, Tracey. How's your _____ new apartment _____ ?
₁

B: Oh, it's a _____ , Marco.
₂

A: Where is it? Is it on a _____ ?
₃

B: Yes, it is.

A: Is it a _____ ?
₄

B: Not really. We just have one _____ , a living room, and a kitchen.
₅

A: That's OK.

B: Yeah. But there's a _____ !
₆

A: Sounds great!

B **Complete the email. Look at the pictures and use the words in the box.**

| small | ~~blue~~ | old | green | large | new | beautiful |

Brian

Hey Dean,

I want to tell you about our new home. It's great! It's a _____ blue _____
₁
house with a(n) _____ garden. It has a(n) _____
₂   ₃
balcony and a(n) _____ living room.
₄
It also has a(n) _____ kitchen but a(n) _____ bathroom.
₅   ₆
And my favorite place in the house is the _____ bedroom.
₇

Come visit soon!

Brian

C **Rewrite the sentences. Use the adjective in parentheses.**

1. Springfield is a town. (beautiful) _____ Springfield is a beautiful town. _____
2. That is a neighborhood. (good) _____
3. I live in a house. (red) _____
4. We have a living room. (nice) _____
5. We have a garden. (large) _____
6. We need a garage. (big) _____
7. It has a kitchen. (great) _____
8. He needs closets. (big) _____
9. I don't want a bedroom. (small) _____

A ▶03-11 Listen to the descriptions. Write the number of the description in the correct box.

 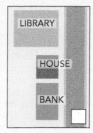    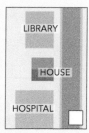

B Complete the sentences with *There's* or *There are*.

1. _____There's_____ a hospital next to the bank.
2. _____ houses near the park.
3. _____ a library down the street.
4. _____ a bank across from the house.
5. _____ a bus stop around the corner.
6. _____ restaurants near the apartment.
7. _____ two drugstores in town.
8. _____ a shopping center on First Street.

C Look at the map. Complete the conversation. Use the prepositions of location from the box. Use some prepositions more than once.

| across from   between   down the street from   next to   around the corner from   near |

Amy: My new apartment is in a great neighborhood.

It's _____near_____ a lot of restaurants.
<u>1</u>

The building is _____ a large park.
<u>2</u>

Brad: Are there any stores near you?

Amy: Yes, there's a small supermarket

_____ my apartment.
<u>3</u>

And there's a large shopping center

_____ the apartment.
<u>4</u>

Brad: Oh, is the shopping center

_____ the bank?
<u>5</u>

Amy: Yes. It's _____ the bank and the
<u>6</u>

drugstore.

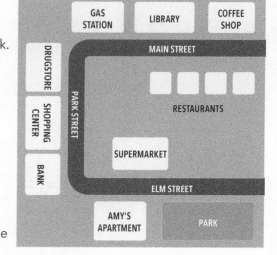

Brad: That's Park Street. You know the gas station on Main Street?

Amy: I think so. It's _____ the drugstore, right?
<u>7</u>

Brad: Right. There are lots of nice restaurants _____ the gas station.
<u>8</u>

There's also a very good coffee shop _____ the restaurants.
<u>9</u>

It's _____ the library.
<u>10</u>

Amy: Cool. Let's have coffee there.

A Complete the questions. Use *Where's* or *Where are.*

1. _____Where's_____ the sink?
2. _____ the stove?
3. _____ the forks?
4. _____ the refrigerator?

5. _____ the spoons?
6. _____ the plates?
7. _____ the microwave?
8. _____ the pots and pans?

B Look at the picture. Complete each conversation. Use *It's* or *They're.*
Use a preposition from the box and the words in parentheses.

in   on   under   over   in front of   behind

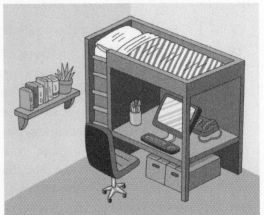

1. A: Where's the desk?

    B: _____It's in the bedroom._____
              (the bedroom)

2. A: Where's the bed?

    B: _____
              (the desk)

3. A: Where are the books?

    B: _____
              (the shelf)

4. A: Where's the chair?

    B: _____
              (the desk)

5. A: Where are the pens?

    B: _____
              (the cup)

6. A: Where's the phone?

    B: _____
              (the computer)

7. A: Where are the boxes?

    B: _____
              (the desk)

C ▶03-18 Listen to the sentences. Check (✓) the picture they describe.

1. a.  ✓   b.  ☐
2. a.  ☐   b.  ☐
3. a. ☐   b. ☐

4. a.  ☐   b.  ☐
5. a.  ☐   b.  ☐
6. a.  ☐   b.  ☐

A Complete the sentences. Write the correct preposition.

1. The test is _____ on _____ Tuesday.
2. Marco's birthday is _____ May 13.
3. The conference calls are _____ 9:30 and 12:00.
4. His classes are _____ Mondays and Wednesdays.
5. The meeting is _____ 2020.
6. Your trip is from June 8 _____ June 12.
7. My English class is _____ night.
8. The party is _____ 12:00 to 6:00.

B Look at the calendar. Complete each question. Use *When's* or *When are*.
Then write an answer. Use the preposition in parentheses.

○ ○ ○

M	**Wed 18**	**Thu 19**	**Fri 20**
A	7:00 a.m.–11:15 a.m. Train to New York	8:00 a.m. Breakfast with Mel	7:30 a.m. Doctor's appointment
R	1:00–3:00 p.m. Design meeting	9:00–9:30 a.m. Design meeting	10:00–11:00 a.m. Online class
C	5:00 p.m. Train home	10:00–11:00 a.m. Online class	3:00 p.m. Phone call with Japan
H		3:00 p.m. Phone call with Japan	

1. A: _____ When's _____ breakfast with Mel?   B: _____ It's at 8:00. _____
   (at)
2. A: _____ the design meetings?   B: _____
   (on)
3. A: _____ the train to New York?   B: _____
   (at)
4. A: _____ the train home?   B: _____
   (at)
5. A: _____ the doctor's appointment?   B: _____
   (on)
6. A: _____ the phone calls with Japan?   B: _____
   (at)
7. A: _____ the online classes?   B: _____
   (from ... to)

C ▶04-06 Listen to the messages. Complete the answers to the questions.

1. A: When's the party?   B: It's _____ at 7:30 _____ .
2. A: When are Sheila's classes?   B: They're _____ today.
3. A: When's Dad's birthday?   B: It's _____ .
4. A: When are the meetings?   B: They're _____ .
5. A: When's the test?   B: It's _____ .
6. A: When's the class?   B: It's _____ .
7. A: When's the appointment?   B: It's _____ tomorrow .
8. A: When are her office hours?   B: They're _____ .

UNIT 4, LESSON 3   THE IMPERATIVE: AFFIRMATIVE AND NEGATIVE

A ▶04-23 Listen to the directions. Circle the imperatives you hear.

1. *(Go)* / *Don't go* straight.
2. *Don't take* / *Take* Exit 5A.
3. *Drive to* / *Cross* the bridge.
4. *Drive* / *Walk* two blocks.
5. *Stop* / *Don't stop* at the traffic light.
6. *Go east* / *Go west* on Route 78.
7. *Turn right* / *Turn left* at the gas station.
8. *Turn right* / *Turn left* at the shopping center.

B Label the pictures. Write affirmative or negative imperatives with words from the box. Use some words more than once.

go straight	stop	turn left	turn right	walk	go

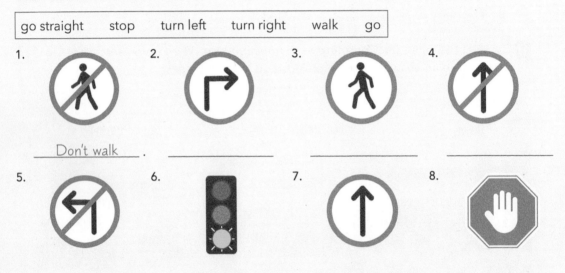

1. ___Don't walk___ .
2. _____
3. _____
4. _____

5. _____
6. _____
7. _____
8. _____

C Look at the map. Complete the directions to White River School. Use the words from the box. Use some words more than once.

Cross	Don't drive	Don't turn left	Walk straight	Turn left	Turn right	Walk

A: How do you get from your house to White River School?

B: Oh, it's very easy. _____Go_____₁ south on Oak Road. _____₂ onto Odell Drive. _____₃ on Odell. _____₄ at Summer Street, that's the way to the park. _____₅ . _____₆ on Post Road. _____₇ the street at the traffic light.

A: Where do I put my car?

B: A car? _____₈ ! _____₉ . It's very close!

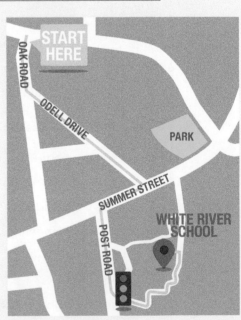

A ▶05-15 **Listen to the conversations. Circle the noun you hear. Underline the irregular plurals.**

1. (watch)   watches
2. child   children
3. dress   dresses

4. scarf   scarves
5. person   people
6. baby   babies

7. woman   women
8. shoe   shoes
9. man   men

B **Look at the website. Complete the sentences. Write the singular or plural form.**

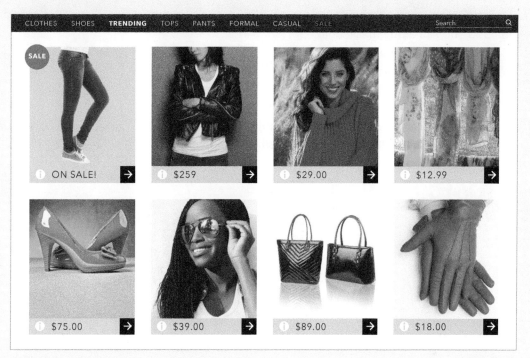

| CLOTHES | SHOES | **TRENDING** | TOPS | PANTS | FORMAL | CASUAL | SALE |

ON SALE! $259 $29.00 $12.99

$75.00 $39.00 $89.00 $18.00

1. The _____jacket_____ is expensive.
2. The _____ are $75.00.
3. The _____ are both black.
4. The _____ are on sale.
5. The red _____ is pretty!

6. The _____ are $39.00.
7. The _____ are many different colors.
8. The _____ are $18.00.
9. This website is for _____ only.

C **Rewrite the sentences. Change the nouns from singular to plural. Make all other changes.**

1. My glove is in my pocket. _____*My gloves are in my pockets.*_____

2. The jacket is only $59. _____

3. The child has a yellow raincoat. _____

4. The woman has a nice watch. _____

5. The tie looks good on the man. _____

6. Where is my black hat? _____

7. The lady needs a pretty dress. _____

8. The shirt is on the shelf. _____

9. Who is the person with a backpack? _____

A ▶06-02 Listen to the conversation between Anna and Joe. Read the sentences. Check (✓) *True* or *False*.

	True	False
1. Joe listens to music on his computer.	☐	✓
2. Anna doesn't like jazz.	☐	☐
3. Joe's brother doesn't play the guitar.	☐	☐
4. Anna likes classical music.	☐	☐
5. Joe and Anna buy music online.	☐	☐
6. Anna watches music videos.	☐	☐
7. Anna doesn't play an instrument.	☐	☐
8. Joe and Anna don't like pop music.	☐	☐

B Look at the music survey. Then complete the sentences. Use the correct form of *love, like,* and *not like.* Use contractions when possible.

Music Survey

	ROCK	POP	JAZZ	HIP-HOP	COUNTRY	R&B
Nina	🙂	🙁	🙁	😍	🙁	🙂
Bill	🙂	😍	🙁	😍	🙁	🙁

🙂 = like   🙁 = not like   😍 = love

1. Nina ___doesn't like___ pop.
2. Bill _____ jazz.
3. Nina and Bill _____ country.
4. Bill and Nina _____ hip-hop.
5. Bill _____ pop.
6. Bill _____ R&B.
7. Nina _____ R&B.
8. Bill and Nina _____ rock.

C Rewrite the sentences. Change affirmative sentences to negative, and negative sentences to affirmative. Use contractions when possible.

1. Sam likes classical music. ___Sam doesn't like classical music.___
2. I listen to a lot of music. _____
3. He likes country music. _____
4. They have a dance party every year. _____
5. Gina doesn't love jazz. _____
6. Edward sings well. _____
7. We play music on our computer. _____
8. You don't need a new phone. _____
9. She doesn't have a lot of songs on her phone. _____

A ▶06-07 Listen to an interview with Lily Warren. Check (✓) the activities Lily and her family do.

	Lily	father	mother	sisters	brother
play the guitar	✓				
play the piano					
do martial arts					
swim					

B Write a short answer to each question. Use contractions when possible.

1. A: Does she play soccer?
   B: Yes, _____she does_____ .

2. A: Do they do martial arts?
   B: No, _____ .

3. A: Do you play an instrument?
   B: No, _____ .

4. A: Does your brother paint?
   B: No, _____ .

5. A: Do you and Amanda cook?
   B: Yes, _____ .

6. A: Do we need our sneakers?
   B: Yes, _____ .

7. A: Does he play guitar?
   B: No, _____ .

8. A: Do they play piano?
   B: Yes, _____ .

C Read the questionnaire. Then write *yes/no* questions and short answers.

TALENT QUESTIONNAIRE Write your name under the talent or hobby.

Ben Derek Victor	Andy Kim	Victor Hana Marco Selena	Pablo Karen	Cindy Hana Karen	Sam Tom

1. Ben and Derek / play a sport
   A: _Do Ben and Derek play a sport?_
   B: _____Yes, they do._____

2. Hana / dance
   A: _____ ?
   B: _____ .

3. Tom and Marco / play an instrument
   A: _____ ?
   B: _____ .

4. Sam / paint
   A: _____ ?
   B: _____ .

5. Karen / sing and dance
   A: _____ ?
   B: _____ .

6. Pablo / paint
   A: _____ ?
   B: _____ .

7. Andy and Kim / play a sport
   A: _____ ?
   B: _____ .

8. Victor, Marco, and Selena / swim
   A: _____ ?
   B: _____ .

UNIT 6, LESSON 3   SIMPLE PRESENT: *WH-* QUESTIONS AND ANSWERS

A ▶06-14 Listen to the questions. Circle the correct answer.

1. (a.) in the evening   b. in bed
2. a. he bikes   b. at the beach
3. a. on the weekend   b. in the mountains
4. a. music videos   b. in my room

5. a. in school   b. in the morning
6. a. in the evening   b. on our balcony
7. a. at 7:00 a.m.   b. in the park
8. a. watch TV   b. the news

B Complete the *wh-* questions. Use the words in parentheses.

A: _____What do you like to do_____
   1 (What / you like to do)
   for fun?

B: Well, I love music.

A: _____
   2 (What music / you like?)

B: Country music.

A: Really? I play country music with my
   sisters and our friend Mateo!

B: _____ ?
   3 (What / you play)

A: I play the guitar.

B: _____ ?
   4 (What / your sisters do)

A: They sing.

B: _____ ?
   5 (What / Mateo play)

A: The drums.

B: _____ ?
   6 (Where / you play)

A: We play in parks. We're at Millburn
   Park tonight. Come!

B: I will! _____
   7 (When / you start?)

A: At 8:30 p.m.

C Complete the conversations. Notice the underlined word or phrase in the answer. Then write the question. Use *What, When,* or *Where.*

1. A: _____Where do you hike_____ ?
   B: I hike <u>in the mountains</u>.

2. A: _____ ?
   B: I exercise <u>on the weekend</u>.

3. A: _____ ?
   B: Ken reads <u>books</u>.

4. A: _____ ?
   B: We play <u>board games</u> with the kids.

5. A: _____ ?
   B: They run <u>in the park</u>.

6. A: _____ ?
   B: Tina watches TV <u>in her bedroom</u>.

7. A: _____ ?
   B: Mika and Sherri go to the movies <u>on Friday nights</u>.

8. A: _____ ?
   B: I listen to <u>rock and pop</u>.

9. A: _____ ?
   B: Dan exercises <u>in the morning</u>.

UNIT 7, LESSON 1   COUNT/NON-COUNT NOUNS; *SOME* AND *ANY*

A ▶07-02 Listen to the sentences. Are the nouns count or non-count? Check (✓) the correct box.

	1	2	3	4	5	6	7	8
Count noun	✓							
Non-count noun								

B Complete the sentences. Use *some* or *any*.

A: What's for breakfast?

B: Hmm. I don't know. Do we have _____any_____ eggs?

                                                                          1

A: Yes, we do. There are _____ eggs on the second shelf in the fridge.

                                                2

B: I need _____ butter and milk, too

                                  3

A: We have butter, but we don't have _____ milk.

                                                                  4

B: Oh. Hmm. Then I'll just make _____ fruit salad.

                                                              5

A: We don't have _____ fruit.

                                        6

B: Yes, we do. There are _____ bananas on the table.

                                              7

A: Right. We *only* have bananas.

B: Never mind then. I'll just have _____ coffee.

                                                            8

A: Well, I'm going shopping! We don't have _____ food.

                                                                          9

C Look at the check. Then answer the questions. Use *some* or *any*.

🏠	John's Café	GUEST CHECK	5 items 🛒
Click an item to modify.		Check number	**8818566**
☑ 2 carrot soup		✏ 🗑	$8.00
☑ 1 chicken sandwich (no onions)		✏ 🗑	$7.25
☑ 1 cheese sandwich (with tomatoes)		✏ 🗑	$7.75
☑ 1 shrimp		✏ 🗑	$17.50
☑ 2 potatoes (side)		✏ 🗑	$6.00
TOTAL			**$46.50**

1. A: Do they want pasta?   B: _____No, they don't want any pasta_____.

2. A: Do they want onions on   B: _____

     the chicken sandwich?

3. A: Do they want shrimp?   B: _____

4. A: Do they want fish?   B: _____

5. A: Do they want chicken soup?   B: _____

6. A: Do they want tomatoes on   B: _____

     the cheese sandwich?

7. A: Do they want potatoes?   B: _____

8. A: Do they want dessert?   B: _____

GRAMMAR PRACTICE   119

A Complete the messages. Use *some* or *any*.

Hi Frida, We need to buy food. I'm at the store. I want chicken for dinner.
Do we have ____some____ ?
1

Hey Andy, That's great. No, we don't have _____ . You need
2
to buy _____ .
3

How about pasta, do we have _____ ?
4

Yes, we have _____ .
5
I need milk for my coffee, do we have _____ ?
6

No, I don't think we have _____ .
7
I'll buy _____ . Anything else?
8

No, that's good. See you later.

B Complete the conversations. Circle the correct word.

1. A: *Can I /* (*Could you*) */ Can we*
      help me?
   B: Yes, of course. What do you need?

2. A: *Can I / Could you / Can we* have a
      piece of cake, please?
   B: Sure, Mark. Here's a piece.

3. A: *Can I / Could you / Can we* bring
      the check?
   B: Sure. Here you go.

4. A: *Can we / Could you / Can I* cut the
      fruit?
   B: No, I don't have a knife.

5. A: *Can I / Could we / Could you* see
      the menus, please?
   B: Yes, ladies. Right away.

6. A: *Can we / Could I / Can you* come
      to the movies, too?
   B: You and Kayla? Sure. I have two
      extra tickets.

7. A: *Could you / Can I / Can we* have
      some tea?
   B: I'm sorry, Beth. There isn't any.

8. A: *Can I / Could you / Can we* finish
      your soup, please?
   B: It's too hot.

9. A: *Can we / Could I / Can you* have a
      burger, please?
   B: Oh, yes. Of course, sir.

C ▶07-18 Listen to the questions. Complete the sentences.

1. _____Could I_____ have some bread, please?

2. _____ come to your party?

3. _____ have a glass of water?

4. _____ email me the picture?

5. _____ get some vegetables?

6. _____ order some dessert, please?

7. _____ bring us some soup?

8. _____ tell me the address of the restaurant?

A ▶08-02 Listen to the questions. Circle the correct answer.

1. (a.) Yes, there is.   b. Yes, there are.   5. a. No, there isn't.   b. No, there aren't.
2. a. No, there isn't.   b. No, there aren't.   6. a. Yes, there are.   b. Yes, there is.
3. a. Yes, there is.   b. Yes, there are.   7. a. No, there aren't.   b. No, there isn't.
4. a. No, there isn't.   b. No, there aren't.   8. a. Yes, there is.   b. Yes, there are.

B Complete the conversation. Use the correct form of *there is / there are*. Use contractions when possible.

A: Excuse me, _____ is there _____ a shopping center near the hotel?
                     1

B: No, _____ . Can I help you with something?
            2

A: Well, I need some clothes and other things, you know, like a toothbrush, shampoo, conditioner …

B: Well, _____ a small store down the street from the hotel. But maybe
            3
_____ things like shampoo and conditioner in the hotel room.
            4

A: No, _____ any deodorant, and _____ any combs or
            5   **6**
hairbrushes in the room.

B: Oh. Well, take the bus to Midtown Crossing. _____ lots of stores there.
                                                      7

A: Oh, one more thing. _____ an ATM near here?
                          8

B: Yes, _____ . It's across from the hotel.
            9

A: Thank you!

C Look at the items in a hotel room. Write questions with *there is* or *there are*. Use the words in parentheses. Write short answers.

1. A: _____ Are there toothbrushes? _____
              (toothbrushes)
   B: _____ Yes, there are _____ .

2. A: _____ ?
             (deodorant)
   B: _____ .

3. A: _____ ?
             (shampoo)
   B: _____ .

4. A: _____ ?
             (body lotion)
   B: _____ .

5. A: _____ ?
             (razors)
   B: _____ .

6. A: _____ ?
             (soap)
   B: _____ .

7. A: _____ ?
             (combs)
   B: _____ .

8. A: _____ ?
             (shaving cream)
   B: _____ .

9. A: _____ ?
             (brushes)
   B: _____ .

A Complete the conversation. Use the correct form of *like*, *want*, or *need* and an infinitive. Use contractions when possible.

A: What do you _____*want to do*_____ tomorrow?
                   1 (want / do)

B: Well, I _____ my sister in the morning. Then I'm free.
          2 (need / call)

A: I _____ to the pool in the morning. I _____ early.
     3 (want / go)   **4 (like / exercise)**

B: Perfect. We can meet after that.

A: What do you _____ ?
                    5 (want / do)

B: I _____ to a museum. Maybe the Museum of Fine Art.
     6 (want / go)

A: Um, no thanks. I _____ at art.
                  7 (not like / look)

B: Oh! We _____ to an art museum. How about a science museum?
         8 (not need / go)

A: Oh, yes I _____ the Museum of Science. I love science.
            9 (want / visit)

B Complete each sentence with the words in parentheses. Write affirmative or negative forms of *need*, *like*, or *want* + infinitive. Use contractions when possible.

1. You _____*don't need to drive*_____ your car. We can take the subway.
          (need / drive)

2. I have a lot of work for tomorrow. I _____ late.
                    (need / stay)

3. Robert _____ elevators. He always takes the stairs.
           (like / take)

4. We _____ lunch tomorrow. Our company always gets pizza on Friday
         (need / bring)
   for everyone!

5. Lucy always leaves for work early. She _____ late.
                         (want / be)

6. They _____ the news. They watch the news online.
           (like / read)

7. Mack _____ a new car. His old car doesn't work.
           (want / buy)

8. You _____ to bed early. The train leaves at 6:00 a.m. tomorrow.
         (need / go)

9. My wife and I eat out a lot. We _____ .
                       (like / cook)

C ▶08-09 Listen to the conversations. Complete the sentences. Use the words in parentheses. Write affirmative or negative forms. Use contractions when possible.

1. The woman _____*needs to park*_____
          (need / park)
   her car.

2. The man _____ in
       (like / exercise)
   the morning.

3. They _____ to the
      (want / go)
   party.

4. She _____ indoors.
      (like / run)

5. They _____ .
         (want / eat out)

6. The woman _____ for a
               (want / go)
   walk in the evening.

7. The man _____ in the rain.
              (like / walk)

8. You _____ for breakfast.
           (need / pay)

UNIT 8, LESSON 3   PREPOSITIONS OF PLACE:
AT, ON, IN

A ▶08-16 Listen to the sentences. Which preposition do you hear? Check (✓) the correct box.

	1	2	3	4	5	6	7	8
at								
on	✓							
in								

B Complete the conversation. Write the correct prepositions: *at, on,* or *in.*

A: Hi, Jenn. Where are you?

B: Hi, Stuart. I'm still _____<u>at</u>_____ school. I'm _____ the library. Where are you?

                                 1   **2**

A: I'm _____ the bus stop, the one _____ the park.

            3   **4**

A: Oh. Do you want to meet _____ the café?

                                  5

B: Flo's Café _____ Second Avenue?

                     6

A: No, Buddy's, around the corner from school, _____ the neighborhood.

                                                                           7

B: Sounds good.

A: Can we meet _____ the front of the café, _____ the left?

                           8   **9**

B: Sure. See you there.

C Write sentences, using the words in parentheses. Use the correct form of the verb.
Add the correct preposition: *at, on,* or *in.*

1. _____ <u>She lives in California</u> _____ .

                                        (she / live / California)

2. _____

                                        (the car / be / the garage)

3. _____

                                        (Tara / live / Korea)

4. _____

                                        (we / work / the third floor)

5. _____

                                        (I / see / Sara / the bus stop)

6. _____

                                        (there / be / an ATM / the corner)

7. _____

                                        (the Chens / live / Sunset Drive)

8. _____

                                        (Louis / run / the park)

9. _____

                                        (the bank / be / 10 Elm Street)

A ▶09-02 Listen to the conversation. Write *this, that, these,* or *those* before each word.

1. _____this_____ desk
2. _____ chairs
3. _____ file cabinet
4. _____ window
5. _____ computers
6. _____ boxes
7. _____ lamps
8. _____ office
9. _____ phone

B Complete the sentences. Use the possessive form of the words in parentheses.

1. What's the _____doctor's_____ name?
   (doctor)

2. Do you have _____ email address?
   (Nick)

3. Where are the _____ jackets?
   (boys)

4. Is this the _____ office?
   (accountant)

5. Where can I find the _____ toys?
   (children)

6. Do you know all the _____ names?
   (students)

7. I never read _____ opinions online.
   (people)

8. Where's _____ car?
   (Dad)

9. Is that your _____ skirt?
   (sister)

C Look at the floor plan. Complete the sentences with the possessive form of the words from the box.

architects   designers   ladies   Lori   manager   men   receptionist   Roman   Nina   Tara

1. _____Tara's_____ desk is near the copy room.

2. The _____ room and the _____ room are across from the receptionist.

3. The _____ desk is very big.

4. The _____ office is next to the copy room.

5. _____ desk is very small.

6. The _____ office has two desks.

7. In the architect's office, _____ desk is near the door.

8. There are file cabinets in the _____ office.

9. The books are in front of _____ desk.

ENTRY

MEN

LADIES

RECEPTIONIST

COPY ROOM

BOOKS

NINA

FILE CABINETS

MANAGER

DESIGNERS

ARCHITECTS

TARA

ROMAN

MIKE

ANDY

CONFERENCE ROOM

LORI   SETH

A ▶09-10 Listen to the questions. Circle the correct answer.

1. **a.** I'm reading the news.   **b.** I read the news.
2. **a.** Yes, I am.   **b.** Yes, I do.
3. **a.** Yes, it works.   **b.** Yes, it's working.
4. **a.** No, I'm not texting.   **b.** No, I don't text.
5. **a.** He's going to the store.   **b.** He goes to the store.
6. **a.** No, it doesn't rain much.   **b.** No, it's not raining now.
7. **a.** No, I don't.   **b.** No, I'm not.
8. **a.** I watch movies.   **b.** I'm watching movies.

B Complete the messages with the present continuous. Use the words in parentheses. Use contractions when possible.

Hey, what ___are you doing___?
1 (you / do)

I _____ to print my homework.
2 (try)
The paper _____.
3 (not / come out)

_____ everything right?
4 (you / do)

Yes, I am. I _____ *print*,
5 (click)
then *OK*. It _____.
6 (not / work)

Maybe change the settings?

I _____ them now.
7 (change)
Still the same.

Well, I _____ my homework.
8 (print)
Email me your homework. I can print it for you.

Really? Oh, thank you! I
_____ it right now.
9 (send)

C Complete the conversations. Notice the underlined word or phrase in the answer. Then write a *wh-* question.

1. A: _____What is he using_____ ?   B: He's using <u>the keyboard</u>.
2. A: _____ ?   B: They're fixing <u>the WiFi</u>.
3. A: _____ ?   B: She's texting <u>her sister</u>.
4. A: _____ ?   B: We're going <u>to the library</u>.
5. A: _____ ?   B: He's wearing a jacket <u>because it's cold</u>.
6. A: _____ ?   B: She's walking <u>to the subway</u>.
7. A: _____ ?   B: Leo is teaching <u>math</u>.
8. A: _____ ?   B: I'm driving <u>Charlie and Owen</u>.
9. A: _____ ?   B: Cole is leaving <u>because he has a class</u>.

A Complete the sentences. Use the prompts.

1. I _____sometimes take a shower_____ at the gym.
   (take a shower / sometimes)

2. She _____ before midnight.
   (goes to bed / rarely)

3. Ed _____ after lunch.
   (brushes his teeth / always)

4. The students _____ on their tablets.
   (read books / often)

5. They _____ .
   (eat pizza / sometimes)

6. _____ together.
   (eat dinner / never / you and Katya)

7. _____ in Arizona.
   (rarely / it / rains)

8. _____ at 7:40.
   (leave the house / usually / I)

9. _____ at a bad time!
   (always / you / call me)

B Complete the sentences using the adverbs of frequency: *always, often, rarely,* or *never.*

1. Paula works very hard. She only relaxes a few hours on Sundays.
   _____Paula rarely_____ relaxes.

2. Peter eats lunch at a restaurant every Tuesday and Thursday.
   _____ eats lunch at a restaurant.

3. Marc only runs at the gym. He doesn't like to run in the park.
   _____ runs in the park.

4. Yuan goes to bed late every night.
   _____ goes to bed late.

5. Yummi eats breakfast every morning, before she goes to work.
   _____ eats breakfast.

6. Hana only goes out for dinner on the first Friday of every month.
   _____ goes out for dinner.

7. Tito never shops in stores. He only shops online.
   _____ shops online.

C ▶09-18 Listen to Ben describe his day. Circle the correct word to complete each sentence.

1. He (never) / sometimes wakes up at 8:00 Monday to Friday.
2. He never / always takes the bus.
3. He never / rarely eats breakfast.
4. He usually / sometimes wears a jacket and tie to work.
5. He often / rarely travels for work.
6. He usually / never goes out for lunch.
7. He rarely / usually stays at work late.
8. He always / sometimes goes to the gym after work.

UNIT 10, LESSON 1   SIMPLE PAST WITH *BE*

A ▶10-02 Listen to the questions. Circle the correct answer.

1. a. Yes, it was.   b. No, they weren't.
2. a. Yes, I was.   b. In 2013.
3. a. No, it isn't.   b. Yes, it was.
4. a. No, it wasn't.   b. Karl.

5. a. Yes, they were.   b. Yes, it was.
6. a. Last weekend.   b. On Main Street.
7. a. No, it wasn't.   b. Yes, it is.
8. a. No, he wasn't.   b. Yes, they were.

B Complete the conversation. Write *was* or *were*.

A: Where _____were_____ you last night?
1

B: The theater.

A: Oh. _____ it good?
2

B: Yes, it really _____ !
3

A: Really? What was the play?

B: *Romeo and Juliet.*

A: Cool. _____ you there with friends?
4

B: Yes, I _____ . Max, Amy, and Ryan _____ there.
5   6

A: Fun. _____ Sam there, too?
7

B: Sam _____ actually *in* the play.
8

A: Really! Wow!

B: Yes. He was Romeo! We _____ really excited.
9

C Complete the conversation. Write questions with *was* or *were*, using the words in parentheses.

1. A: _____Was the weather good_____ ?   B: Yes, it was.
   (the weather / good)

2. A: _____ ?   B: Good, thanks!
   (how / your weekend)

3. A: _____ ?   B: No, I wasn't. I was on a bike trip.
   (you / home)

4. A: _____ ?   B: In Accord, New York.
   (where / the bike trip)

5. A: _____ ?   B: Yes, we were.
   (you / at Pine Park)

6. A: _____ ?   B: Yes, it was.
   (it / beautiful)

7. A: _____ ?   B: Terri, Josh, Taylor, and some other people.
   (who / with you)

8. A: _____ ?   B: Yes, it was. But I was tired!!
   (it / relaxing)

9. A: _____ ?   B: Because we were on our bikes all day!
   (why / you tired)

A ▶10-07 Listen to the questions. Circle the correct answer.

1. a. No, he doesn't. (b.) No, he didn't.
2. a. Yes, she does. b. Yes, she did.
3. a. No, they don't. b. No, they didn't.
4. a. Yes, we do. b. Yes, we did.

5. a. No, you didn't. b. No, you don't.
6. a. Yes, I did. b. Yes, I do.
7. a. Yes, it does. b. Yes, it did.
8. a. No, we didn't. b. No, we don't.

B Complete the conversation. Use the simple past form of the verbs in parentheses.

A: Hey, Marta. Are you OK?

B: Yeah, I'm just tired!

A: Oh, too much fun this weekend?

   ___Did you dance___ all night?
   1 (you / dance)

B: No, I didn't. I _____ home
   2 (stay)
   and _____ the house!
   3 (clean)

A: All weekend?

B: Well, I _____ in the yard,
   4 (work)
   too. And I _____ two cars
   5 (wash)
   and two dogs!

A: _____, too?
   6 (you / cook)

B: No, I didn't. Not in my clean kitchen!
   How was your weekend?

A: I _____ my friends
   7 (visit)
   in the city.

B: _____?
   8 (you / go out)

A: Yes, we did.

B: So *you* _____ all night!
   9 (dance)

A: Yes, I did. It was great!

C Look at the list of things to do on Nazir's phone. Which things did he finish today?
Write *yes/no* questions and answers. Use the words in parentheses.

1. A: ___Did Nazir return the books to the library?___
      (return the books to library)
   B: ___Yes, he returned the books to the library___.

2. A: _____
      (call his parents)
   B: _____

3. A: _____
      (paint the garage)
   B: _____

4. A: _____
      (clean the kitchen)
   B: _____

5. A: _____
      (wash the car)
   B: _____

6. A: _____
      (help Annie with homework)
   B: _____

7. A: _____
      (work in the yard)
   B: _____

8. A: _____
      (fix the computer)
   B: _____

● ● ●	10:01	▭
‹ menu	Checklist	add ⊕

Things to do

✓ return books to the library
✓ clean kitchen
   wash car
   work in yard
✓ call parents
   fix computer
✓ help Annie with homework
   paint garage

UNIT 10, LESSON 3 SIMPLE PAST: *WH-* QUESTIONS AND IRREGULAR VERBS

A ▶10-15 Listen to the sentences. Are they in the present or past? Check (✓) the correct box.

	1	2	3	4	5	6	7	8
Present								
Past	✓							

B Complete the email. Use the correct form of the verbs in parentheses.

New email

From: Tanya Hart To: Melissa@georgio.com Mom Gina@Home.com Date: August 3

Hi, all.

We came back from vacation last night. It was great! We _____flew_____
1 (fly)
to Madrid and then we _____ the train to Portugal.
2 (take)
We _____ so many things along the way. The ocean in
3 (see)
Portugal was beautiful. We _____ every day. One day
4 (swim)
we _____ shopping. We _____ some great
5 (go)   **6 (meet)**
people. Everyone was kind and friendly and made us feel at

home. The food was so good! In Portugal we _____
7 (eat)
a lot of fish. I even _____ lessons on how to cook
8 (get)
fish! We really _____ a relaxing vacation!
9 (have)
Have a look: VacationPics / Tom&Tanya.

Love, Tanya

C Complete the conversations. Notice the underlined word or phrase in the answer. Then write a *wh-* question.

1. A: Where did you go to school? _____ B: I went to school in Cali.
2. A: _____ ? B: I met the manager.
3. A: _____ ? B: They went to Canada.
4. A: _____ ? B: I gave Sue my notes because she needs to study.
5. A: _____ ? B: I took photographs on vacation last month.
6. A: _____ ? B: I came by car.
7. A: _____ ? B: I bought the sweater online.
8. A: _____ ? B: I took Mr. Potter to the airport.
9. A: _____ ? B: Sara ate an apple.

GRAMMAR PRACTICE 129

REFERENCES

▶11-01 ALPHABET

Aa	Bb	Cc	Dd	Ee	Ff	Gg	Hh	Ii	Jj	Kk	Ll	Mm
Nn	Oo	Pp	Qq	Rr	Ss	Tt	Uu	Vv	Ww	Xx	Yy	Zz

▶11-02 CARDINAL NUMBERS

1	2	3	4	5	6	7	8	9	10
one	two	three	four	five	six	seven	eight	nine	ten
11	**12**	**13**	**14**	**15**	**16**	**17**	**18**	**19**	**20**
eleven	twelve	thirteen	fourteen	fifteen	sixteen	seventeen	eighteen	nineteen	twenty
21	**22**	**23**	**24**	**25**					
twenty-one	twenty-two	twenty-three	twenty-four	twenty-five					

30	40	50	60	70	80	90
thirty	forty	fifty	sixty	seventy	eighty	ninety

100	200	300	400	500	600	700	800	900
one hundred	two hundred	three hundred	four hundred	five hundred	six hundred	seven hundred	eight hundred	nine hundred

1,000	5,000	10,000
one thousand	five thousand	ten thousand

100,000
one hundred thousand

1,000,000
one million

1,000,000,000
one billion

▶04-02 ORDINAL NUMBERS

1st first	2nd second	3rd third	4th fourth	5th fifth
6th sixth	7th seventh	8th eighth	9th ninth	10th tenth
11th eleventh	12th twelfth	13th thirteenth	14th fourteenth	15th fifteenth
16th sixteenth	17th seventeenth	18th eighteenth	19th nineteenth	20th twentieth
21st twenty-first	22nd twenty-second	23rd twenty-third	24th twenty-fourth	25th twenty-fifth
26th twenty-sixth	27th twenty-seventh	28th twenty-eighth	29th twenty-ninth	30th thirtieth
40th fortieth	50th fiftieth	60th sixtieth	70th seventieth	80th eightieth
90th ninetieth	100th hundredth			

▶04-03 MONTHS OF THE YEAR

January	February	March	April
May	**June**	**July**	**August**
September	**October**	**November**	**December**

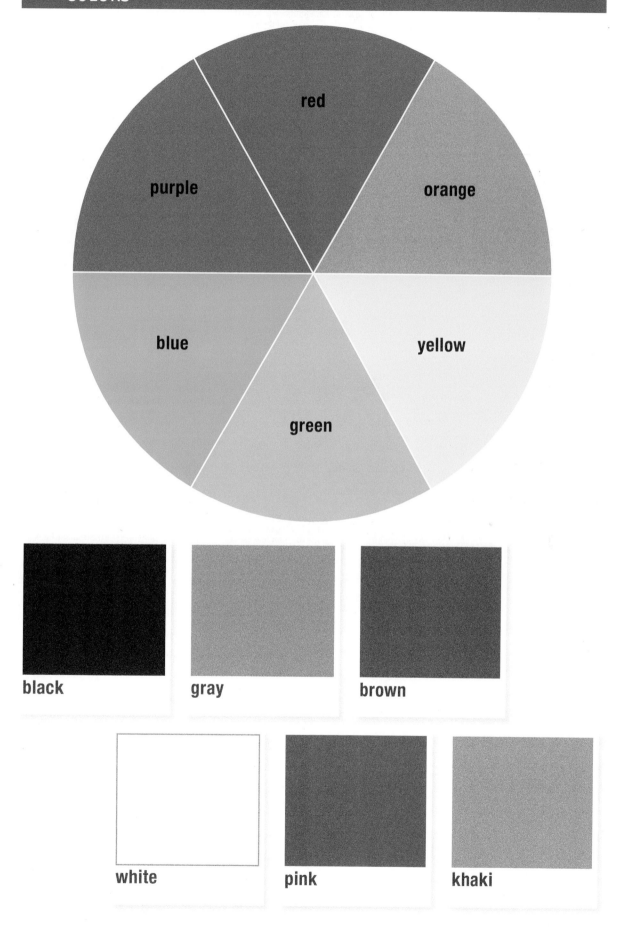

red

purple

orange

blue

yellow

green

black

gray

brown

white

pink

khaki

Photo Credits

Welcome unit

Page 2: VGstockstudio/Shutterstock; 3 (front cover): Klaus Vedfelt/Getty Images; 4 (all images): Pearson Education, Inc.

Unit 1

Page 5: Paul Bradbury/Caiaimage/Getty Images; 5 (bottom, right): Pearson Education, Inc.; 6 (top, right): Pearson Education, Inc.; 6 (top): Sam Edwards/OJO Images/Getty Images; 6 (left): LightField Studios/Shutterstock; 6 (center): Gstockstudio/123RF; 6 (right, top): Kzenon/Shutterstock; 6 (right, bottom): Iakov Filimonov/123RF; 7: Pearson Education, Inc.; 8 (top): Pearson Education, Inc.; 8 (top row, architect): Cyberstock/Alamy Stock Photo; 8 (top row, manager): Michal Kowalski/Shutterstock; 8 (top row, chef): Wavebreak Media/Alamy Stock Photo; 8 (top row, engineer): P.studio66/Shutterstock; 8 (top row, dentist): Hero Images/Getty Images; 8 (top row, flight attendant): David Lyons/Alamy Stock Photo; 8 (bottom row, doctor): Lightwave/123RF; 8 (bottom row, programmer): PR Image Factory/Shutterstock; 8 (bottom row, nurse): Shutterstock; 8 (bottom row, scientist): Alexander Raths/Shutterstock; 8 (bottom row, accountant): PeopleImages/iStock/Getty Images; 8 (bottom row, illustrator): Slaven/Shutterstock; 9: Pearson Education, Inc.; 10 (top): Pearson Education, Inc.; 10 (computer): Tetra Images/Alamy Stock Photo; 10 (phone): Kraisak Srisodkeaw/123RF; 10 (desk): John_Kasawa/iStock/Getty Images; 10 (printer): StockPhotosArt/Shutterstock; 10 (pen): Phant/Shutterstock; 10 (pencil): Christophe Testi/Shutterstock; 10 (chair): Luisa Leal Photography/Shutterstock; 10 (notepad): Gerald Bernard/123RF;10 (cell phone): Saginbay/Shutterstock; 10 (eraser): Yurakp/123RF; 10 (sticky note): Cloki/Shutterstock; 10 (cabinet): Hurst Photo/Shutterstock; 11 (computer): Scanrail/123RF; 11 (printer): Robert Milek/Shutterstock; 11 (smartphones): Oleksiy Mark/Shutterstock; 11 (office phone): Ilya Genkin/Shutterstock; 11 (chair): Kirill Cherezov/123RF; 11 (cabinet): Fransiska Indromojo/123RF; 11 (desk): Margo Harrison/Shutterstock; 11 (notepads): Lamb/Alamy Stock Photo; 11 (pencils): Patrick Samuels/Shutterstock; 11 (pens): Sergii Moskaliuk/123RF; 11 (sticky notes): Serezniy/123RF; 12 (top): Pearson Education, Inc.; 12 (bottom, left): Pearson Education, Inc.; 12 (bottom, center): Pearson Education, Inc.; 12 (bottom, right): Pearson Education, Inc.; 14 (top): Miya227/Shutterstock; 14 (center): Pook_jun/Shutterstock.

Unit 2

Page 15 (family photo on smartphone and background): iStockPhoto/Getty Images; 15 (hands holding smartphone): Blackzheep/Shutterstock; 15 (bottom, right): Pearson Education, Inc.; 16 (top): Pearson Education, Inc.; 16 (left): Shutterstock; 16 (right, bottom): Shutterstock; 16 (right, top): Shutterstock; 17: Pearson Education, Inc.; 18 (top): Pearson Education, Inc.; 18 (top row, left): Kues Images/Shutterstock; 18 (top row, center left): Paffy/Shutterstock; 18 (top row, center): Blend Images/Shutterstock; 18 (top row, right): Olegdudko/123RF; 18 (bottom row, left): Antonio Guillem/123RF; 18 (bottom row, center): Javi Indy/Shutterstock; 18 (bottom row, right): Nestor Rizhniak/Shutterstock; 19: Pearson Education, Inc.; 20 (top): Pearson Education, Inc.; 20 (Will): Goodluz./Shutterstock; 20 (Karen): Mimagephotography/Shutterstock; 20 (Mia): Victoras/Shutterstock; 20 (Brad): Ostill/123RF; 20 (Linda): Believeinme33/123RF; 20 (Meg): Andersonrise/123RF; 20 (Luke): Domenicogelermo/123RF; 20 (Ana): Cathy Yeulet/123RF; 20 (Sam): Racorn/123RF; 20 (Delia): Ana Bokan/Shutterstock; 20 (Ron): Wavebreakmediamicro/123RF; 21: Pearson Education, Inc.; 22 (top): Pearson Education, Inc.; 22 (left): Hero Images Inc./Alamy Stock Photo; 22 (center): MBI/Alamy Stock Photo; 22 (right): KidStock/Blend Images/Getty Images; 24: Sfio Cracho/Shutterstock.

Unit 3

Page 25: Westend61/Getty Images; 25 (bottom, right): Pearson Education, Inc.; 26 (top): Pearson Education, Inc.; 27: Pearson Education, Inc.; 28 (top): Pearson Education, Inc.; 29: Pearson Education, Inc.; 30 (top): Pearson Education, Inc.; 30 (left): Artazum/Shutterstock; 30 (right, top): Essential Image Media/Shutterstock; 30 (right, bottom [table setting]): Africa Studio/Shutterstock; 30 (right, bottom [white cup in table setting]): Maria Komar/Shutterstock; 31 (left): PPA/Shutterstock; 31 (center): PercivalSantamaria/Istock/Getty Images; 31 (right): Iriana88w/123RF; 32 (top): Pearson Education, Inc.; 32 (apartment complex): Jessicakirsh/Shutterstock; 32 (living room): Katarzyna Bialasiewicz/123RF; 32 (kitchen): Blend Images/Alamy Stock Photo; 33 (left): Katarzyna Bialasiewicz/123RF; 33 (center left): Artazum/Shutterstock; 33 (center right): Zhu Difeng/Shutterstock; 33 (right): Artazum and Iriana Shiyan/Shutterstock; 34 (top): JP WALLET/Shutterstock; 34 (bottom): Thiti Sukapan/Shutterstock.

Unit 4

Page 35: Dominic Blewett/Alamy Stock Photo; 35 (bottom, right): Pearson Education, Inc.; 36 (top): Pearson Education, Inc.; 37: Pearson Education, Inc.; 38 (top): Pearson Education, Inc.; 38 (top row, left): Hongqi Zhang/123RF; 38 (top row, center left): Vtls/Shutterstock; 38 (top row, center right): EpicStockMedia/Shutterstock; 38 (top row, right): Scanrail/123RF; 38 (bottom row, left): Vectorfusionart/Shutterstock; 38 (bottom row, center left): Shutterstock; 38 (bottom row, center right): Blend Images/Shutterstock; 38 (bottom row, right): Shutterstock; 39: Pearson Education, Inc.; 40 (top): Pearson Education, Inc.; 40 (top row, left): Antonio Balaguer Soler/123RF; 40 (top row, center left): Tupungato/Shutterstock; 40 (top row, center): Alina Streltsova/Shutterstock; 40 (top row, center right): Tycson1/Shutterstock; 40 (top row, right): 4kclips/Shutterstock; 40 (bottom row, left): Rainer Lesniewski/Alamy Stock Photo; 40 (bottom row, center left): Conceptw/123RF; 40 (bottom row, center): Jojoo64/123RF; 40 (bottom row, center right): Mr. Alien/Shutterstock; 40 (bottom row, right): Kaolen/Shutterstock; 42 (top): Pearson Education, Inc.; 42 (center): James Kirkikis/Shutterstock; 44: Mariola Anna S/Shutterstock.

Unit 5

Page 45: Luay Bahoora/Alamy Stock Photo; 45 (bottom, right): Pearson Education, Inc.; 46 (top): Pearson Education, Inc.; 46 (bottom row, left): Flashon Studio/Shutterstock; 46 (bottom row, center left): Karkas/Shutterstock; 46 (bottom row, center): Oleksii Demidov/123RF; 46 (bottom row, right): Superstock/Alamy Stock Photo; 46 (bottom row, center right): Adisa/Shutterstock; 46 (top row, left): Kirill Vorobyev/Shutterstock; 46 (top row, center left): Pixelrobot/123RF; 46 (top row, center): Igor Grochev/Shutterstock; 46 (top row, center right): Satina/123RF; 46 (top row, right): Coprid/Shutterstock; 47: Pearson Education, Inc.; 48 (top): Pearson Education, Inc.; 48 (center, right): Pincarel/Shutterstock; 49 (winter): Loinok Sawai/Shutterstock; 49 (spring): Khathar ranglak/Shutterstock; 49 (summer): SFL Travel/Alamy Stock Photo; 49 (fall): James Nesterwitz/Alamy Stock Photo; 49 (dry season): Fotos593/Shutterstock; 49 (wet season): Eteri Okrochelidze/Shutterstock; 50 (top): Pearson Education, Inc.; 50 (left): Denisfilm/123RF; 50 (center, left): Alexfan32/Shutterstock; 50 (center): Iryna Kalchenko/123RF; 50 (center, left): Alexfan32/Shutterstock; 50 (center, right): Viorel Sima/Shutterstock; 50 (right): Baona/iStock/Getty Images; 51 (left): Pearson Education, Inc.; 51 (left): Pearson Education, Inc.; 52 (top): Pearson Education, Inc.; 54: Africa Studio/Shutterstock.

Unit 6

Page 55: Andresr/E+/Getty Images; 55 (bottom, right): Pearson Education, Inc.; 56 (top): Pearson Education, Inc.; 56 (top row, left): Kzenon/Shutterstock; 56 (top row, center left): Stokkete/123RF; 56 (top row, center right): Zamfir Cristian/123RF; 56 (top row, right): Stockyimages/Shutterstock; 56 (bottom row, left): Pavel L Photo and Video/Shutterstock; 56 (bottom row, center left): Richard Sowersby/REX/Shutterstock; 56 (bottom row, center right): Ysbrand Cosijn/Shutterstock; 56 (bottom row, right): Radius images/Getty Images; 57: Pearson Education, Inc.; 58 (top): Pearson Education, Inc.; 58 (top row, guitar): Leungchopan/Shutterstock; 58 (top row, piano): Mike Booth/Alamy Stock Photo; 58 (top row, take pictures): Iakov Kalinin/Shutterstock; 58 (top row, write): Gstockstudio/Shutterstock; 58 (top row, soccer): Shawn Pecor/Shutterstock; 58 (top row, basketball): Dotshock/123RF; 58 (bottom row, cook): lenetstan/Shutterstock; 58 (bottom row, paint): Pressmaster/Shutterstock; 58 (bottom row, dance): Dmitriy Shironosov/123RF; 58 (bottom row, sing): Ferli Achirulli/123RF; 58 (bottom row, swim): Maridav/Shutterstock; 58 (bottom row, martial arts): Andrii Kaderov/123RF; 59: Pearson Education, Inc.; 60 (top): Pearson Education, Inc.; 60 (bottom row, left): Andrey_Popov/123RF; 60 (bottom row, center left): Wavebreakmedia/Shutterstock; 60 (bottom row, center right): Takayuki/Shutterstock; 60 (bottom row, center): Syda Productions/Shutterstock; 60 (bottom row, right): Jovanmandic/iStock/Getty Images; 60 (top row, left): Stockbroker/123RF; 60 (top row, center left): Jacek Chabraszewski/Shutterstock; 60 (top row, center): GaudiLab/Shutterstock; 60 (top row, center right): Jacek Chabraszewski/Shutterstock; 60 (top row, right): Holbox/Shutterstock; 61: Pearson Education, Inc.; 62 (top): Pearson Education, Inc.; 62 (center, left): Jacob Lund/Shutterstock; 62 (center, right): Wavebreakmedia/Shutterstock; 64 (bottom): Wavebreak Media ltd/Alamy Stock Photo; 64 (top): Maria Maarbes/Shutterstock.

Unit 7

Page 65: Andresr/E+/Getty Images; 65 (bottom, right): Pearson Education, Inc.; 66 (top): Pearson Education, Inc.; 66 (top row, banana): Maks Narodenko/Shutterstock; 66 (top row, apple): Vaclav Volrab/Shutterstock; 66 (top row, orange): Valentyn Volkov/Shutterstock; 66 (top row, beef): Margouillat photo/Shutterstock; 66 (top row, pork): Bernd Juergens/Shutterstock; 66 (center row, potato): Freer/Shutterstock; 66 (center row, onion): Valentyn Volkov/Shutterstock; 66 (center row, carrot): Olinchuk/Shutterstock; 66 (center row, tomato): Fedorov Oleksiy/Shutterstock; 66 (center row, chicken): Jiang Hongyan/Shutterstock; 66 (center row, turkey): Tjp55/Shutterstock; 66 (bottom row, cheese): Nattika/Shutterstock; 66 (bottom row, milk): Sommai/Shutterstock;66 (bottom row, butter): Pairoj Sroyngern/Shutterstock; 66 (bottom row, fish): OnlyFOOD/Shutterstock; 66 (bottom row, shrimp): Piyaset/Shutterstock; 67: Pearson Education, Inc.; 68 (top): Pearson Education, Inc.; 68 (hamburger): Foodandmore/123RF; 68

(sandwich): Rafa Irusta/Shutterstock; 68 (pizza): Nikolay Pozdeev/123RF; 68 (salad): Johnfoto18/Shutterstock; 68 (french fries): Yellow Cat/Shutterstock; 68 (bread): Baibaz/Shutterstock; 68 (pasta): Joe Gough/Shutterstock; 68 (rice): Elena Elisseeva/Shutterstock; 68 (coffee): Anatoly Tiplyashin/Shutterstock; 68 (tea): Maxfeld/Shutterstock; 68 (soda): M. Unal Ozmen/Shutterstock; 68 (juice): Evgeny Karandaev/Shutterstock; 69: Pearson Education, Inc.; 70 (top): Pearson Education, Inc.; 70 (menu): Helmut Meyer zur Capellen/imageBROKER/Alamy Stock Photo; 70 (napkin): 5 second Studio/Shutterstock; 70 (check): Feng Yu/123RF; 70 (tip): Andrey_Popov/Shutterstock; 70 (ice): Praisaeng/Shutterstock; 70 (sugar): Edie Layland/123RF; 70 (salt): Ruslan Kudrin/Shutterstock; 70 (pepper): Aaron Amat/Shutterstock; 70 (ketchup): Kornienko/123RF; 70 (linen background): EasterBunny/Shutterstock; 71 (top): Pearson Education, Inc.; 71 (bottom): Rido/Shutterstock; 72 (top): Pearson Education, Inc.; 72 (left): Rawpixel.com/Shutterstock; 72 (right, top): Ionia/Shutterstock; 72 (right, bottom): Joshua Resnick/123RF; 74: microstockasia/123RF.

Unit 8

Page 75: August_0802/Shutterstock; 75 (bottom, right): Pearson Education, Inc.; 76 (top): Pearson Education, Inc.; 76 (top row, body lotion): Itorn/123RF; 76 (top row, toothbrush): Olga Popova/123RF; 76 (top row, shampoo): Olga Popova/123RF; 76 (top row, liquid soap): SzaszFabian Ilka Erika/Shutterstock; 76 (top row, bar soap): Jiri Hera/Shutterstock; 76 (top row, conditioner): Siraphol/123RF; 76 (top row, toothpaste): Milos Luzanin/123RF; 76 (bottom row, comb): Winai Tepsuttinun/Shutterstock; 76 (bottom row, brush): Dulcenombre Maria Rubia Ramirez/123RF; 76 (bottom row, tissues): IS200807/Image Source/Alamy Stock Photo; 76 (bottom row, shaving cream): George Tsartsianidis/123RF; 76 (bottom row, razor): Aurelio Scetta/123RF; 76 (bottom row, deodorant): Aragami12345/123RF; 77: Pearson Education, Inc.; 78 (top): Pearson Education, Inc.; 78 (top row, parking lot): BestPhotoPlus/Shutterstock; 78 (top row, cafe): Eviled/Shutterstock; 78 (top row, restroom): Kostsov/Shutterstock; 78 (top row, fitness center): Edvard Nalbantjan/123RF; 78 (center row, pool): Kosmos111/Shutterstock; 78 (center row, gift shop): Tooykrub/Shutterstock; 78 (center row, business center): RosalreneBetancourt 11/Alamy Stock Photo; 78 (center row, sauna): Konstantin Labunskiy/123RF; 78 (bottom row, lobby): 36clicks/123RF; 78 (bottom row, escalator): Peekhawfang Samarn/Shutterstock; 78 (bottom row, elevator): Dejan Krsmanovic/123RF; 78 (bottom): Anna Zakharchenko/123RF; 79: Pearson Education, Inc.; 80 (top): Pearson Education, Inc.; 80 (top row, stadium): Blaz Kure/Shutterstock; 80 (top row, art gallery): NagyBagoly Arpad/Shutterstock; 80 (top row, subway station): Gwoeii/Shutterstock; 80 (top row, museum): Shutterstock; 80 (center row, theater): Fer Gregory/Shutterstock; 80 (center row, bank): David R. Frazier Photolibrary, Inc./Alamy Stock Photo; 80 (center row, ATM): Bankerwin/123RF; 80 (center row, convenience store): RosalreneBetancourt 5/Alamy Stock Photo;80 (center row, post office): Nick Maslen/Alamy Stock Photo; 80 (bottom row, department store): JN/Alamy Stock Photo; 80 (bottom row, airport): Sagase48/Shutterstock; 80 (bottom row, hair salon): Gemenacom/Shutterstock; 80 (bottom row, club): Marko Poplasen/Shutterstock; 82 (top): Pearson Education, Inc.; 82 (left): Zhu Difeng/Shutterstock; 82 (center): August_0802/Shutterstock; 82 (right): Shen Max/Shutterstock; 84 (top): Tekkol/Shutterstock; 84 (center): Top Photo Engineer/Shutterstock.

Unit 9

Page 85: Chaay_Tee/Shutterstock; 85 (bottom, right): Pearson Education, Inc.; 86 (top): Pearson Education, Inc.; 86 (center, left): Jakub Gojda/123RF; 86 (center, middle): MaraZe/Shutterstock; 86 (center, right): Artsplav/Shutterstock; 86 (top row, old): Scanrail/Shutterstock; 86 (top row, new): Patryk Kosmider/Shutterstock; 86 (top row, fast): Alexey Kuznetsov/123RF; 86 (top row, slow): Joy Brown/Shutterstock; 86 (top row, heavy): Ljupco Smokovski/Shutterstock; 86 (top row, light): Daniel M Ernst/Shutterstock; 86 (bottom row, noisy): Ronald Sumners/Shutterstock; 86 (bottom row, quiet): Jacob Lund/Shutterstock; 86 (bottom row, hard): Lightwise/123RF; 86 (bottom row, soft): Sukpaiboonwat/Shutterstock; 86 (bottom row, small): Venus Angel/

Shutterstock; 86 (bottom row, big): Nuwat Chanthachanthuek/123RF; 87: Pearson Education, Inc.; 88 (top): Pearson Education, Inc.; 88 (top row, tablet): Mr. Aesthetics/Shutterstock; 88 (top row, laptop): Igor terekhov/Alamy Stock Photo; 88 (top row, powercord and plug): Robert Babczynski/Shutterstock; 88 (top row, headphones): Stockforlife/Shutterstock; 88 (top row, cable): Mrs. Nuch Sribuanoy/Shutterstock; 89: Pearson Education, Inc.; 90 (top): Pearson Education, Inc.; 90 (top row, left): Ana Blazic Pavlovic/123RF; 90 (top row, center left): Tetra Images/Shutterstock; 90 (top row, center right): Merla/Shutterstock; 90 (top row, right): Imagehit Limited|Exclusive Contributor/123RF; 90 (center row, left): Michaeljung/Shutterstock; 90 (center row, center left): Stockyimages/Shutterstock; 90 (center row, center right): Leung Cho Pan/123RF; 90 (center row, right): Inti St Clair/Blend Images/Getty Images; 90 (bottom row, left): Fabrice Lerouge/Onoky/Getty Images; 90 (bottom row, center left): Rawpixel.com/Shutterstock; 90 (bottom row, center right): Syda Productions/Shutterstock; 90 (bottom row, right): Tetra Images/Getty Images; 92 (top): Pearson Education, Inc.; 92 (center): Rawpixel/123RF; 94: Design Exchange/Shutterstock.

Unit 10

Page 95: Jordan Siemens/Taxi/Getty Images; 95 (bottom, right): Pearson Education, Inc.; 96 (top): Pearson Education, Inc.; 97: Pearson Education, Inc.; 98 (top): Pearson Education, Inc.; 98 (top row, left): Racorn/123RF; 98 (top row, center left): Choreograph/123RF; 98 (top row, center): Katarzyna Bialasiewicz/123RF; 98 (top row, center right): Vlue/Shutterstock; 98 (top row, right): Iakov Filimonov/123RF; 98 (bottom row, left): Michaeljung/Shutterstock; 98 (bottom row, center left): Arek_malang/Shutterstock; 98 (bottom row, center): Africa Studio/Shutterstock; 98 (bottom row, center right): Konstantin Chagin/Shutterstock; 98 (bottom row, right): Maridav/Shutterstock; 99: Pearson Education, Inc.; 100 (top): Pearson Education, Inc.; 100 (top row, left): Bodrumsurf/Shutterstock; 100 (top row, center left): Melvyn Longhurst/Alamy Stock Photo; 100 (top row, center right): Juice Images/Alamy Stock Photo; 100 (top row, right): 2p2play/Shutterstock; 100 (center row, left): Pressmaster/Shutterstock; 100 (center row, center left): Iakov Kalinin/Shutterstock; 100 (bottom row, left): RosalreneBetancourt 3/Alamy Stock Photo; 100 (bottom row, center left): Shutterstock; 100 (bottom row, center right): Image Source/Alamy Stock Photo; 100 (bottom row, right): Ekaterina Pokrovsky/123RF; 102 (top): Pearson Education, Inc.; 102 (left): BlueOrange Studio/Shutterstock; 102 (center): Graham Mulrooney/Alamy Stock Photo; 102 (right): Wildroze/E+/Getty Images; 104: Antonio Guillem/Shutterstock.

Grammar Practice

Page 105 (top row, left): Shutterstock; 105 (top row, center left): Anatoliy_gleb/Shutterstock; 105 (top row, center right): El Nariz/Shutterstock; 105 (top row, right): Africa Studio/Shutterstock; 105 (center row, left): David R. Frazier Photolibrary, Inc/Alamy Stock Photo; 105 (center row, center left): Rawpixel.com/Shutterstock; 105 (center row, center right): Fancy Yan/DigitalVision/Getty Images; 105 (center row, right): Chombosan/Shutterstock; 105 (bottom row, left): Zivica Kerkez/Shutterstock; 105 (bottom row, center left): Andrey_Popov/Shutterstock; 105 (bottom row, center right): Pressmaster/Shutterstock; 105 (bottom row, right): Nd3000/Shutterstock; 105 (bottom): Wavebreakmedia/Shutterstock; 107 (top): Shutterstock; 107 (Robert): Diego Cervo/Shutterstock; 107 (Anna): ESB Professional/Shutterstock; 107 (Lisa): SpectralDesign/Shutterstock; 107 (Tim): ESB Professional/Shutterstock; 107 (Emily): Nadino/Shutterstock; 107 (John): Rido/Shutterstock; 107 (Will): Rido/Shutterstock; 107 (Carol): Iko/Shutterstock; 107 (Maria): ESB Professional/Shutterstock; 107 (Stephan): Digital Media Pro/Shutterstock; 108: Jetta Productions/Getty Images; 115 (top row, left): Africa Studio/Shutterstock; 115 (top row, center left): Odua Images/Shutterstock; 115 (top row, center right): Izabela Magier/Shutterstock; 115 (top row, right): Jose Angel Astor/123RF; 115 (bottom row left): Val Thoermer/123RF; 115 (bottom row, center left): Rohappy/Shutterstock; 115 (bottom row, center right): Nadiia Korol/Shutterstock; 115 (bottom row right): Art_photo_sib/Shutterstock; 129: Pawel Kazmierczak/Shutterstock.

Illustration Credits

418 Neal (KJA Artists), John Goodwin, Phil Hackett (both Eye Candy Illustration), Anjan Sarkar (Good Illustration)